D0153734

The Leaf Book *and the* Crossed Wood

A thought provoking study on the effects of the Bible and the Cross in an
isolated culture in which they had never been previously introduced.
Based on the true story found in *Prophecies of Pale Skin*

D.S. Phillips

Copyright © 2014, D.S. Phillips

All rights reserved. No part of this book may be reproduced, stored, or transmitted by any means—whether auditory, graphic, mechanical, or electronic—without written permission of both publisher and author, except in the case of brief excerpts used in critical articles and reviews. Unauthorized reproduction of any part of this work is illegal and is punishable by law.

ISBN 978-0-9885450-3-8

For my third son, Lazarus Tyndale.
May our Great Creator do a miracle in your
heart and open up your spiritual eyes to see
and cherish Him alone as your Greatest
Treasure. May the Crossed Wood become
your greatest passion and the Leaf Book
alone become your ultimate foundation.

If it isn't worth dying for, is it really worth living for to begin with?

- **D.S. Phillips**

CONTENTS

INTRODUCTION

The Leaf Book and the Crossed Wood, these are two things that were non-existent in the Dao culture until the year 2007. It had been around 2000 years since the cross of Jesus Christ first made its groundbreaking mark on humankind but these people were still living and dying in the remote jungles of Indonesia with not the slightest clue as to who Jesus was or that He had even existed at all.

Theirs was an unwritten dialect of language, existing only in the spoken word, handed down from generation to generation through the daily lives, stories, legends and incantations of their people and nothing more. Their Creator's story, the pages and words of the Bible also were unknown to them and had no bearing on their people or culture. In fact, when the Dao did finally see a Bible for the first time they did not know what to call it so they borrowed a word from a neighboring language: "*kapoge*". In the Dao language pronounced "kapo-iye" meaning "a sheet" (kapo) of "leaves" (iye).

Little did they know that this "leaf book" as they would call it, and the "crossed-wood" of this Man that they would come to love would have an awe-inspiring effect on their people group that would change them forever. They would never be the same. And not only would the Dao tribe never be the same but neither would the two young travelers that had carried these things to them from the other side of the world.

My hope is that as you follow this study you also, like the Dao people, will be both challenged and changed in some way by the Leaf Book and the Crossed Wood that so many of the people of this remote tribe in the jungles of Indonesia have come to cherish.

How This Study Works

There are fifteen days to this study and each day is based on one of the fifteen chapters from the book *Prophecies of Pale Skin.* You can do this study alone or it can be done in a daily or weekly group setting and be used as a conversation guide. Each day will include a scripture passage relating to the chapter being discussed, a thought provoking study, and a series of questions relating to the chapter. Throughout this book and in each chapter you will also find a number of quotes that have been taken directly from the book *Prophecies of Pale Skin.* This is so that each topic and study can be effectively related to a real life context and situation.

Even though you may not be the one with a machete in hand, cutting through the jungle to find a new unreached tribe, even though you may not be the one sitting in a small, humid, thatch roofed hut in the middle of nowhere trying to translate God's Word into a new language in which it has never been translated, you still have a very important role to play in this awesome task called missions. My prayer is that God will use this study in your life, to help you gain a growing passion to be a part of the awesome things He is doing in this world in our generation.

DAY

I

WHAT *is* YOUR GREATEST JOY?

"The water I give people takes away thirst altogether. It becomes a perpetual spring within them, giving them eternal life."

John 4:14

Day 1: What Is Your Greatest Joy?

Perhaps you have heard the famous old saying by missionary Jim Elliot "He is no fool who gives what he cannot keep to gain what he cannot lose". Not long after writing those words Jim Elliot, along with his companions, were murdered by the spears of the very men they had come to minister to. He knew the risks before he ever stepped foot into those jungles. He knew that he was laying down what he could not keep anyways. He knew that if he was to lose his life something far greater awaited him beyond this life that no jungle spear, tropical sickness or any earthly thing could threaten to take away. And so he made the best investment that an individual can possibly make and embraced with open arms what ultimately he could not lose.

If Jim Elliot was right, what do his words imply about the man or woman who does the opposite? What about the person that doesn't spend his life for a worthy cause? What about the man that doesn't invest his life, doesn't lay it down for this ultimate treasure that he cannot lose? What about the man that spends his life investing in one thing after another that he cannot keep? The individual that spends nearly all of his waking minutes, days and hours just trying to get a little bit more and a little bit more of what he will be forced to abandon. The one that day after day invests in and hoards and stores and claws for just one more bit of what he will ultimately leave behind.

What did Jesus say about such an individual? In Luke 12:16-21 Jesus tells a short story to His disciples about His perception of such a man. *"A rich man had a fertile farm that produced fine crops. In fact, his barns were full to overflowing. So he said, 'I know! I'll tear down my barns and build bigger ones. Then I'll have room enough to store everything. And I'll sit back and say to myself, 'My friend, you have enough stored away for years to come. Now take it easy! Eat, drink, and be merry!' "But God said to him, 'You fool! You will die this very night. Then who will get it all?'* Jesus didn't beat around the bush when He spoke of this type of man to His disciples. "You fool!" He says in reference to the individual that hoards and hoards for the future and puts everything he has into his own bigger barns and bigger houses and bigger savings and more resources for his own personal comfort.

But isn't this nearly an exact description of the type of attitude and perspective that fills our society and is even accepted in our churches today? It's all about retirement, the 401k, the hundreds of thousand or even millions of dollars that I will live off of when I am old. And even worse, the church itself sets the model for this type of mindset with its multi-million dollar buildings, mega-churches and five hundred dollar suit-wearing preachers leading the way. *"You Fool!"* Jesus says. Don't you understand that every single bit of it will be left to someone else? Don't your realize that your are wasting your life on something that you cannot keep!

Missionaries such as Jim Elliot and those individuals that are even today laying it all on the line for the spread of the gospel and living day in and day out wherever they are at for the spreading of the glory of God in their communities are simply those that have realized a very simple truth. The truth that, the joy that awaits us at the end of the race, whenever that may be, is far greater than any lesser joy that a life can be invested in.

"Wikipai had made the long hike down to Taomi not merely to represent his people to the outsiders for the sake of material gain but mainly to begin teaching his people about a new talk that they had not yet heard. He wanted the people that had gathered there to also hear the things he had heard about the great Creator Spirit. With his whole heart he desired for them also to know about the words of the leaf book that had changed him and revolutionized his life. Wikipai knew that what his people ultimately needed was not the leaf paper money of the outsiders. There was way more at stake than just material gain. They needed the words from the leaf book of the Creator One even more. He had set out to bring them these words." - From page 11 of *Prophecies of Pale Skin*

"With the little bit of strength he had remaining Wikipai motioned to us he wanted to speak. Very slowly and in almost a whisper he began: *"Oh friend, do not cry for me. Do not cry for me. Yes, it is true that my body is wasting away. I am like a jungle stream that has not been fed by the rain for many days. But although my body is very weak, my spirit is strong. I know what the Great Creator One's Son has done for me. And if I die here in this place, then that is what the Creator One has chosen for me. I am ready to go. Do not cry for me.""*- From page 14 of *Prophecies of Pale Skin*

We still have doubts and fears, days of discouragement and trials but deep down inside we know that what we will experience in the future and are already beginning to experience is the first tastes of an Ultimate Treasure that we welcome with open arms. A Joy that we cannot lose even in death!

Questions

1. What are you living for?

2. Is the thing that you are living for something that you cannot lose?

3. Is the thing that you are spending your days on and centering your weeks around something that you are willing to die for?

4. What if you found out at this very moment that tomorrow was your day of death. Would you look back with regret on what you have invested your life in up to this point?

*Read **Luke 12:33-34** and ponder these verses and how they relate to your own life

DAY

2

WHAT *is* YOUR SOURCE *of* HOPE?

"He saved us, not because of the good things we did, but because of his mercy. He washed away our sins and gave us a new life through the Holy Spirit. He generously poured out the Spirit upon us because of what Jesus Christ our Savior did."

Titus 3:5-6

Day 2: What Is Your Source Of Hope?

Why is it that there are so many places in this world that have seemingly been "evangelized" or "missionized" but have not yet been genuinely changed by the message of the cross? Is there a type of man-centered evangelization running rampant in our day and age which *"has a form of godliness but denies its power"*? (2 Timothy 3:5) Is there a form of missions being carried across the world and to other places which teaches people to attend services at a church building every week "to please God" and wear the right clothes to "look their best for Jesus" and pray the right prayers to "invite Jesus to come into your heart" but, which is centered on man instead of Christ? A system which is centered on man and his ability to save himself through his actions instead of being centered on Jesus Christ Himself and the work that He alone could have done through His life, death, burial and resurrection?

> "Why is it never enough? How come I am never any better off after I pray this 'Sinner's Prayer'?" I wondered time and time again why I couldn't experience the reconciliation and freedom from fear and guilt that I longed for. I was a young teenager and there was no one that could give me an answer. Every Sunday my God-fearing parents would make sure my two brothers and I were in the local church. Every week I would sit in the church feeling the weight of God's judgment crushing down on me, knowing deep down inside that even though I knew the right answers in Sunday School, I didn't have a clue who the real God of the Bible was or what He or She might be like. - From page 19 of *Prophecies of Pale Skin*

A "salvation" experience which places man and his ability at the center of the stage instead of Jesus Christ and His sacrifice for sins is not a true salvation at all because it magnifies the creation instead of the Creator. Many of our churches are filled with people that are just like I was; people that are following a form of godliness that they have been taught since they were small children but have never truly experienced the freedom from fear and reconciliation with God that can only truly come through the work of Jesus Christ Himself. People that have placed their hope in something that can never save them.

> "Just repeat this little prayer after me" the preacher said once again. "I pray this prayer and repeat these words every Sunday! Nothing ever changes! I still feel the same!" I thought to myself... "But maybe this time it will finally work. If I pray this prayer of penance just one more time maybe I will be spared," I reasoned with myself. I will try again just this one last time. *"Dear Jesus, I ask you to please come into my heart. I invite you to come into my life. I want to go to heaven...Amen."* Even after I was done praying I kept my eyes squeezed shut, waiting, hoping that something would happen. Perhaps it had worked? Perhaps I had right then and there finally been "saved". Maybe I would finally feel different this time? I hoped with everything in me that God was finally seeing me as one of His own. As the days went on however those old familiar feelings of guilt and judgment weighed down on me once again. It often seemed I couldn't even look up towards the sky without being reminded that there is a great big God above those skies, looking down at me, poised and ready to cast me into the hellfire at any moment. Nothing was different. Everything was still the same. This "Sinner's Prayer" had failed me once again. - From page 21 of *Prophecies of Pale Skin*

Many of today's churches are filled with people that have ultimately put their hope in themselves, not in the work and person of Jesus Christ. People that sometimes are even willing to *"travel over land and sea to win a single convert, and when he becomes one, you have made him twice as much a son of Hell as you are"* (Matthew 23:15)

The Lord is not limited to our understanding and ways. If He wants to, He can even use a jackass to get His point across! (Numbers 22:21-41) But often times, the places that experience truly God-glorifying, Christ-exalting missions work are the places that have been taught by a messenger who has himself experienced the life-giving Christ-centered miracle of salvation first in his own heart. A miracle that God must get the glory for because He is the only one that can open our spiritual eyes to see the truth. A miracle that Jesus must get the credit for because He is the One and only spotless Lamb of God that could have become the sacrifice for sin on our behalf. And a miracle that can only come through the power of Holy Spirit because He is the only One that can draw us to the Father and cause us to understand the work of Jesus Christ.

Mr. Moyer continued "If you are trusting in anything at all to get you to Heaven in addition to Jesus Christ alone and His finished work on the cross on your behalf, then you are looking straight into the face of God and telling Him that what His Son Jesus did on the cross isn't good enough. You are telling God that He might as well not have sent His son Jesus at all." That statement got my attention...suddenly I realized what the problem had been all these years...all along, since I was just a kid in Los Angeles, I had been trying to gain acceptance with God through a man made ritual called the "Sinner's Prayer". All these years I had been trying over again and again to say these special words just right, just as the preacher had told me to say them. My faith never had been, even the tiniest bit, in the finished work of this man Jesus Christ. In that moment I was faced with the dark realization that I had been deceived. My whole life I had been trying to gain God's approval through a decoy that could never be anything but a shallow substitute for the real thing. Though I knew about Jesus and even many of the right answers about Him, my trust was in a man-made Christian church ritual that could never save me. - From page 32 of *Prophecies of Pale Skin*

The true salvation experience hinges on His work, not on ours. That is why salvation is a miracle. It is an event which man himself does not have the ability in his natural state to usher in. Jesus said in John 6:44 *"No one can come to me unless the Father who sent me draws him"* God does the drawing so only God Himself can get the glory from any true salvation experience. That is why man and his ability cannot be on center stage in the salvation experience or in truly God-glorifying, Christ-exalting missions work.

No longer could I, in the words of Mr. Moyer "look in the face of God and tell him that His son Jesus' sacrifice on the cross is not enough". I knew I needed to trust in what Jesus had done for me, not in anything I had done or any special magical words I had spoken in hopes of gaining His approval... Tears began rolling down my face as this realization sank in. For the first time I felt the presence of God's Spirit inside of me. Chills shot down my spine and the hair stood up on the back of my neck as I felt the burden of judgment and sin that I had carried for so long lifted off of my shoulders. I had been in church my whole life but that was the day God decided to open my eyes... There wasn't a doubt in my mind from that day forward that I was forgiven. The weight of fear and judgment that I had carried around with me as long as I could remember was gone. Jesus Christ had succeeded where the "Sinner's Prayer" had failed. - From page 34 of *Prophecies of Pale Skin*

Questions

1. If right now someone asked you the question "How do you know you are going to heaven?" what would your reply be? Would it be "because I prayed......." or because I.........." or would it be "because of what Jesus has done.....". In other words, what is your salvation experience centered on-your ability or Christ's ability?

2. Is it possible for someone to grow up in the church knowing all of the correct answers about Jesus Christ but to never have truly placed his or her trust in the finished work of Jesus Christ himself?

3. Why do you think there are so many cities, towns and places around the world that have "a form of godliness" but have never truly experienced the God-glorifying gospel that places Jesus Christ Himself on center stage?

4. What do you think is the criteria for God-glorifying, Christ-centered missions and evangelization. Do you as an individual and the church you attend keep Christ on center stage? Or has a form of man-centered jargon worked its way into your own life, family and church?

5. If a man-centered gospel has shown itself to be the center of my own salvation experience or the method of evangelization and missions that are being put forward in my church, what needs to happen to put the finished work of Jesus Christ and Jesus Himself back on center stage where He belongs?

* Read **1 Corinthians 15:1-5** and ponder these verses and how they relate to your own life.

DAY

3

WHAT *is*
GOD'S AGENDA?

"Go and make disciples of all the nations,
baptizing them in the name of the Father
and the Son and the Holy Spirit.
Teach these new disciples to obey
all the commands I have given you.
And be sure of this: I am with you always,
even to the end of the age."

Matthew 28:18-20

Day 3: What Is God's Agenda?

Does God have a clear and concise agenda for this world? Does He have an intricate plan in mind that He has been bringing together since before He ever created even a single atom or molecule? Does He have a clear-cut goal which He has laid out for us in scripture and which ultimately cannot fail because He will see it through to completion? Or is God more the type that doesn't really have a plan at all? A Being that has perhaps created all the elements and spun them into action to where this world could begin but Who is now just sitting on the sidelines depending on us to make the ultimate difference? Is He, the great God and most powerful Being in the universe, merely sitting on His throne up in heaven at this very moment biting His nails and nervously tapping His foot, just hoping that we will be obedient enough to where His hopes for this world can finally come together someday?

If we really do believe that God is the most powerful being in the universe, that He has complete power and authority over all of Creation, and that we belong to Him, then these are very important questions. In the Christian circles that I grew up in, not only was man wrongfully placed on center stage in the process of salvation but man was also placed on center stage in many other facets as well. Even after I had finally realized my own need for Christ's sacrifice for sins on my behalf and had trusted in Him alone for my salvation the thick entangling sludge of a man-centered view of God and His agenda for my life was constantly surrounding me even in the Christian colleges, schools and churches that I attended.

> I had thought a lot about what I should do with my life... Some of the professors at the schools I attended suggested to the other students and myself that we should try to figure out what *"God's call"* for our life was and go from there...By what my teachers at school were telling me, it seemed that I should base what I would do with my life on my own interests and what I liked to spend my time doing. My main passion since I had been a young teen in California seemed to have been skateboarding so it only made sense that this must be what God wanted me to center my life around. - From page 43 of *Prophecies of Pale Skin*

Over and over again I was told that my desires and my comfort were King, that what I wanted to do with my life should be centered on me, not anyone or anything else.

In Romans 15:20-22 the Apostle Paul makes some very intriguing statements about why he was doing what he was doing with his life and why he was going where he was going. *"My ambition has always been to preach the Good News where the name of Christ has never been heard, rather than where a church has already been started by someone else.* **I have been following the plan spoken of in the Scriptures**, *where it says, "Those who have never been told about him will see, and those who have never heard of him will understand." In fact, my visit to you has been delayed so long because I have been preaching in these places."*

According to Paul, God does have a clearly defined plan and agenda for this world; a plan which Paul quotes from Isaiah 52:15, a plan which was already out in the open long before Paul himself ever stepped foot on the earthly scene. This is why Paul's ambition was to first go to the places where literally *"...the name of Christ has never been heard"* and where there has not yet been *"...a church already started"*. This prophecy from the prophet Isaiah was far more than just a good idea or one of the various options out there that Paul could choose from. It was the very plan of God Himself, clearly laid out in the Scriptures! It became Paul's ultimate ambition to see this prophecy fulfilled.

I encountered a man that said something very different from what I had heard up to that point concerning finding "God's call"... He had recently returned from the South Pacific Islands and I will never forget those letters he brought with him. Stacks of letters from tribal people begging for someone to come and live with them and teach them about their Creator...He made copies of the letters and handed them out in class. I couldn't believe what I was reading. "We want to know how to go to God's good place after we die. We don't want to go to the place of fire but we have no one to teach us. Please send someone quickly before too many more of us die!" one letter said. Another letter described the Good News of eternal life as "a big jar of sweet, delicious cookies" that we Americans and Westerners are "keeping all for ourselves because they are so good that we don't want to share." - From page 45 of *Prophecies of Pale Skin*

And now, in our day and age, nearly two thousand years after Paul walked the earth and according to scholars, close to 3,000 years since Isaiah first uttered this prophecy under the guidance of God's Spirit around the 8th century BC, these words still remain unfulfilled.

So if God does have a clear plan for this world, an agenda clearly lined out in scriptures that says *"Those who have never been told about him"* should have an opportunity to see, *"and those who have never heard of him"* should have an opportunity to understand shouldn't we, just like Paul and so many other New Testament saints, run hard towards those places where as Paul described *"the name of Christ has never been heard"* and there has not yet been a single *"church already started"*?

Up until that point I had been completely confident in what I believed God's call and purpose was for my life and I was more than comfortable with the thought of skateboarding the rest of my life away in California while sharing about Jesus with people there. Mr. Gordy handed out to everyone in the class a form, which he called "The Great Commission Exemption Form". It had all kinds of thought provoking statements in it like "If you believe that everything that Jesus teaches in the Bible applies to you EXCEPT for His command in Matthew 28 to *'Go into all the world and preach the gospel to EVERY creature'* please check this box and sign your name here." Many of the other students and even some of my close friends got so angry about the things that he said during that specific class and those "Great Commission Exemption Forms". It was as if they felt threatened by it all. Like their thoughts and dreams of Christian coffee shops and Christian t-shirt companies and being in a Christian rock band and whatever else were being threatened right before their eyes. For me however, it was a week that turned my whole world upside down and that I felt absolutely liberated by. It was that week that I realized for the first time that the infamous "Call of God" that I had so often heard about in my previous college classes was not something that I had to wait for. It was something that I already had. Something that was written down in ink and that I already had in my hands! - From page 46 of *Prophecies of Pale Skin*

Ultimately, only you can decide whether or not you will follow God's command to "GO". Perhaps you would rather follow the example of Jonah and run the opposite direction for the sake of your own comfort, but in the end there are only three options for the follower of Christ; you can either "go" just like so many of the great saints before us, you can do everything in your power to send others and support them in this awesome task just like so many in the New Testament church of Paul's day, or you can be one of the disobedient. There is no other option for a true follower of Christ.

> I was not exempt from Jesus command to "go into ALL the world" any more than any of my fellow classmates were. These words of Jesus applied to all of us and if I truly claimed to follow the teachings of Jesus, I should be just as ready to follow these words as any other words He said. I couldn't just pick which of Jesus' teachings and commands I liked, or that I felt fit my own plans and scrap the rest!... I didn't want to support any longer such a mass hoarding of spiritual truth in the midst of such a big world, much of it starving for just a few crumbs that we might drop from our big truth drenched American tables. - From page 47 of *Prophecies of Pale Skin*

Questions

1. What is God's clear-cut agenda for this world according to Isaiah 52:15 and Romans 15:20-12?

2. Is what I am doing with my life centered on my own agenda for my life and my own measly likes and dislikes? Or is my life centered around God's agenda for the spread of His glory in this world?

3. Is there any part of my life where I am picking which of Jesus' teachings and commands fit my own plans and scrapping the rest? Am I living as though I am exempt from certain things that Jesus said because I am uncomfortable with doing what He asks of me?

4. If my life has been ultimately ordered around my own comfort and plans instead of around God and His agenda for this world what does this say about my view of God?

5. If a man-centered view and agenda is dominating my life and God's agenda for this world is not important to me, what needs to be changed in my life and perspective to where God and His glory are placed back on center stage?

* Read **Matthew 28:18-20** and ponder these verses and how they relate to your own life

DAY

4

WHAT *is* HE WORTH?

"Be very glad, because these trials will make you partners with Christ in his suffering, and afterward you will have the wonderful joy of sharing his glory when it is displayed to all the world."

1 Peter 4:13

Day 4: What Is He worth?

One of the greatest deterrents to missions and going to the hard places for the sake of the gospel in the modern day church is our fear of suffering. We are in a love affair with our comfort. We have succumbed to the lie that God's ultimate goal for His followers is their own prosperity and lack of suffering. We have plunged so deeply into our man-centered view of God that we think all He exists for is to make ME happy. We have wrongfully set ourselves up in such a way that we are living as if we ourselves are the center of God's universe. We do not care about His agenda for this world but instead think God exists to serve us, our desires and our plans.

For some of us, good health and lack of disease or sickness has become our ultimate idol, which we place on the mantle of our minds and live for every day. Others of us bow down daily to the god of wealth and prosperity and see church and prayer merely as a daily avenue to more riches and a bigger house and a more expensive car and nicer clothes and a more extravagant weekend getaway. Others of us pay homage to the god of friends, co-workers and even family. We live for the approval of others and find our happiness and worth in the praise of the person to our right or left or in attaining the next ring on the social or professional ladder.

Whichever one it is, whatever god it is that we have wrongfully set up behind all the facades of spirituality and church attendance, if that god is threatened, we are ready to bail all together. Our ultimate desire that has become even more important to us than God Himself has been threatened. And so even though we may be willing to keep attending church and playing Christian, we want nothing to do with the type of gutsy Jesus-following that says "Jesus, I will give anything to follow you, I will do anything to see you glorified, I will go anywhere to make you known".

This is why there are not more missionaries being sent out to the last unreached, hard to get to remote areas in this world and to the hard to reach Muslim nations of our generation. We are more ready to send bombs and soldiers to many of these people and places than we are to send the gospel and missionaries. Why?

Because they threaten our biggest priority. They threaten us with suffering. They have the possibility of disturbing what has become the most important to us, our ultimate idol - our comfort.

> We were sat down to the announcement that Muslim factions, some with ties to extremist Muslim groups that also had a presence in Indonesia, had just hijacked airplanes and flown them into the twin towers in New York City...Not long afterwards we received word that there had been explosions on two different islands in Indonesia. One in a major tourist area had been planted with intent of killing Americans and other westerners and another had been planted at the entrance to the American Embassy in Indonesia's capital, Jakarta. Fighting had broken out on other predominantly Muslim islands as well and the few followers of Jesus that there were in Indonesia were being tortured and decapitated for their faith. We were only months away from leaving for Indonesia and all the sudden we were hit with the stark realization that this was not a game..."What is our message really worth?" I began asking myself... But it had been the same for this Man we claimed to follow. Jesus Himself had come to this world knowing what would happen to Him from the beginning. He knew He would be tortured and murdered on possibly the cruelest device invented by man... Still, He came anyways." - From page 57 of *Prophecies of Pale Skin*

Jesus, in his humanity also faced situations where He had to choose in between His own comfort and suffering for the sake of the advancement of the message of the cross. He cried out with tears to His Father the evening before His crucifixion saying *"everything is possible for you. Please take this cup of suffering away from me. Yet I want your will, not mine."* (Mark 14:36) Jesus did not want to face suffering any more than we do, but His attitude was such that He placed His Father's agenda above His own and as a result was willing to purchase our ultimate treasure through the very sufferings that He asked His Father to take away!

> God never assured us that our worst fears wouldn't come true, but as we continued to wrestle with these fears He reminded us that He isn't just the God of America. He is the God of the universe. Even with all the other things we would be leaving behind, we would never be leaving Him behind. He would be with us every step of the way and there was nowhere we could go where He wasn't already. Through our doubts and fears, through any hardship or trial we might face He would be with us in it all. - From page 60 of *Prophecies of Pale Skin*

> God's Son Himself had to make the decision to leave the most perfect and comfortable of all places as He said goodbye to living with His own Father in order to come and minister to people like us. He faced the most gruesome trials and torture of all kinds and He knew that it was all going to happen to Him, but He came anyways. We came to the conclusion that because there was no turning back for Him, there could be no turning back for us... The enchanting land of Indonesia had become like a set of gallows to us, but boy were they beautiful gallows. They were nearly irresistible. - From page 61 of *Prophecies of Pale Skin*

There is a reason that Jesus chose suffering over His own comfort. *"He was willing to die a shameful death on the cross because of the joy he knew would be his afterward."* (Hebrews 12:2) He knew that the joy awaiting him on the other side of that suffering far outweighed any amount of joy He could experience through a lack of suffering or through making His own comfort top priority. He was holding out for the greatest pleasure that no one and nothing else could give Him besides His own Father. To Him, it would be well worth it!

> Looking out the front window of the house and towards the main road I could see people walking by the front gate one at a time all going in the same direction... I realized that the strange singing I was hearing was in Arabic. It was the Muslim call to prayer. All of these people were walking to the local mosque at 4:30 in the morning to pray. Within minutes we could hear hundreds, maybe even thousands of loudspeakers ringing out from all over the city, one in every neighborhood calling their faithful followers to morning prayer. Each one of these thousands of people were responding to these Arabic calls before the sun was even up. It was something that they did nearly every day...They also had their traditions, hopes, fears and questions. They had their prayers and rituals that they held onto and placed their hope in, just like I had grown up and held on to my prayers and rituals back in America. They also had their ways of trying to escape God's judgment, their special words that they repeated five times every day in hopes of being set free from their fear of hell... As different as I was from these people, I realized that when it came down to spiritual things, we were the same, looking for the same thing. They were searchers. They needed Jesus just as much as I needed Him. They needed to be set free from their rituals and incantations and special words of religion, just as much as I had needed to be set free from the rituals and decoys I had been taught as a child. - From page 73 of *Prophecies of Pale Skin*

Only when we see God for whom He really is, our Ultimate Treasure that no other thing can even hold a candle to, will we finally be willing to place all other lesser joys on the altar for the sake of the advancement of the gospel. Only when we finally smash the idols of comfort and safety and take our own health and wealth off of the throne that Jesus belongs on in our lives, will we finally be able to say "Yes Jesus, I believe you are worth it! I will give anything to follow you, I will do anything to see you glorified, I will go anywhere to make you known".

Questions

1. What are some of my own greatest fears? Do I have fears that are keeping me from going where God may have me to go?

2. What are some of my greatest priorities and joys in this life? If God Himself is not my greatest joy am I willing to sacrifice any lesser joys for the sake of His glory in and through my life?

3. If I claim to be a follower of Jesus what should my view be of suffering? What was Jesus' attitude towards suffering the cross?

4. What is my attitude towards Muslim nations and unreached people of other religions? Do I view them with compassion as people in need of a Savior or do I hate them as enemies?

5. If God Himself is not my greatest Joy and my own comfort and safety have become idols in my life, what needs to change in my view and priorities to where I can take on the attitude of Christ?

* Read **Hebrews 12:1-4** and ponder these verses and how they relate to your own life.

DAY

5

WHAT WILL
it COST?

"You are all children of God through faith in Christ Jesus. And all who have been united with Christ in baptism have been made like him. There is no longer Jew or Gentile, slave or free, male or female. For you are all Christians; you are one in Christ Jesus."

Galatians 3:26-28

Day 5: What Will It Cost?

What will it cost us to gain credibility with the suffering people that we have hopes of ministering to? We can start by asking the question "What did it cost Jesus to identify with us in our humanity?"

He became one of us. He walked among us. He left behind a place and position of comfort and perfection. He lived in a place with no pain, no hunger, no physical hardship and traded it in for a place filled with sickness, pain, suffering and not even *"a place to lay his own head"* (Luke 9:58).

But why would he leave behind a place with so much to offer Him to come to a place with so little? For the glory of His Father and the love of His sheep. (John 17&20) And the very reason we can now see him as someone who can identify with our joys and sorrows and gains and losses is because He embraced the pains and sufferings of humanity with open arms. Now we likewise can embrace Him as someone that understands us and the trials that we face. He genuinely loves us to the point that He would even endure the tortures and physical pains of this world and the cross for our spiritual wellbeing!

> "My name is Fernando Hutajulu!" he continued and went on to tell us about how his people used to be cannibals and the very first group of Germans that had ever come to his tribe were murdered and then eaten by his grandparents and family. He continued, "More Germans came after we ate those first ones though! The people of my tribe were completely bewildered as to why more of these white skinned foreigners would continue coming to us even after some of them had been killed and eaten. So eventually we listened to the message that the foreigners brought and now most of my tribe are believers in Jesus. They remain followers of Jesus to this day despite the fact that much of Sumatra is predominantly Muslim" Fernando excitedly told us. - From page 82 of *Prophecies of Pale Skin*

When we, on the other hand, do the opposite of this Man we claim to follow and run from the sufferings that God has sovereignly appointed in our lives for His own glory and the spread of His kingdom, often times we are running from the very thing that gives us credibility with the suffering people that we are trying to minister to.

It is when those that are watching us see that we are willing to leave everything behind and make sacrifices and endure hardship and suffer for the sake of our message that they begin to understand that we ourselves really do believe the words we have come to tell them. They begin to see that this message of the cross and Jesus Himself really are our Greatest Possession!

If Jesus really is our Greatest Treasure and we truly do understand that no trial of hardship can befall us that our loving King hasn't sovereignly ordained for our good and His glory among the nations then it will affect us and change us.

> We glanced behind us on the left to see a teenage girl with severely deformed legs using her hands to drag herself along. She was able to make it to the edge of the small group gathered and she began to join us in singing. Her mouth and the muscles in her face seemed contorted as she tried to sing along and the sounds coming from her mouth were strange and off pitch but she closed her eyes and half smiled as she continued to sing. As the father of the house dealt out the rice into separate bowls and carefully made sure that everyone got at least a small portion, the crippled girl motioned to Fernando that she had something to say. Fernando leaned over and translated from Indonesian to English in a whisper so that we also could understand. The girl slurred her words as she struggled to speak... "I have been looking forward to this ever since I heard you were coming. I do not have many things that I can enjoy in this life. But one thing that I can enjoy is singing to our God. I am just so, so happy to be gathered together with you all tonight. It brings me so much joy to get together and sing praises to our King. Thank you so much for visiting with us." she concluded as she looked over at Jennie and I with a sweet, contorted smile and tears in her eyes. - From page 87 of *Prophecies of Pale Skin*

If we walk as changed men and women we will be willing to back up our words with our actions and will encourage others to do so also, not tear them down on the basis of gender or color or social status when they step out and choose the hard road and the un-trodden path for the sake of the advancement of the gospel.

> "These jungle trails and mountains are no place for a woman!...I have seen places like these and hiked trails like this. It would be nearly crazy to take Jennie along don't you see?" he continued... But even if she was alone and there was no one else at all to go with her, I knew that she would be hiking the jungle trails by herself if she had to!... She then started in to her soft-spoken yet very sincere reply..."I have trained and waited for a long time now to go on this survey. I know I will struggle! You don't have to tell me that I will be the slowest one on the trail! Don't you think I know these things? But don't you think that when the people and specifically the Dao women see me struggling on the trail and they see the sweat pouring from my face and perhaps even see me in pain from the journey to get to them, then they will understand all the more in the future what our message is worth to me? I want the women of the Dao tribe both young and old also to know that this is a message for them, not just the men of the tribe. I want them to see in my life that the message we bring is for everyone, man or woman! That is why I am going on this survey, the hardship is worth it to me!" she concluded. - From pages 109-112 of *Prophecies of Pale Skin*

We should be willing not only to endure suffering but should see it is a privilege and opportunity to share in the sufferings of Jesus Himself. We should embrace the awesome truth that Jesus Himself is worth far more than any pleasure we could experience, worth more than any lesser treasure that we could leave behind in order to make Him known. Then people will begin to see the difference in our lives, namely that our hope is in something different than comfort and security and health and wealth and the preservation of our own wellbeing. And some of those that are watching us may even begin to ask questions about the hope that we have and the reason that we do what we do and live the way that we live. Then we will *"be ready to give an answer to those that ask the reason for the hope that we have"* (1 Peter 3:15).

Questions

1. What did Jesus leave behind for the advancement of the Gospel? What did He leave behind to embrace us as part of God's family?

2. Should I as a follower of Jesus expect to leave behind any less for the sake of God's glory and the advancement of the gospel in the remaining unreached places where *"Christ has not yet been named and that have not a single church"* (Romans 10:20)?

3. What stories from the Bible make you feel the most like you can identify with Jesus in His humanity? Why do those specific stories and passages stick out to you?

4. Can you think of an instance in your life where you were able to minister to someone because they had seen you go through a hard situation or circumstance? Why did that person see you as someone they could come to? What was it that gave you credibility with them to where they came to you to be ministered to?

5. What was Jesus' attitude towards those that would have and did discourage Him from taking the hard road and enduring hardship for the glory of His father and advancement of the cross? (Read Matthew 4:1-10, 16:23.)

6. Has there been a time in your life when you have been discouraged by others from doing what you know God wants you to do on the basis of gender, race, age or social status? If so, what should your attitude be towards taking the easy way out for the sake of your comfort instead of doing what you know God wants you to do?

* Read **Matthew 16:24-26** and ponder these verses and how they relate to your own life.

DAY

6

DOES GOD KNOW WHAT HE *is* DOING?

"God deliberately chose things the world considers foolish in order to shame those who think they are wise. And he chose those who are powerless to shame those who are powerful."

1 Corinthians 1:27-28

Day 6: Does God Know What He is Doing?

Over and over again we read stories in the Bible of inadequate people doing mind-blowing things for the glory of God. From the story of Moses, the murderer that was *"slow of speech"* (Exodus 4:10), being used of God to deliver the Israelite slaves out of the hand of the mighty Egyptians, to the classic example of David the shepherd boy taking down the gargantuan giant of a man, Goliath (1 Samuel 17).

From God's own son Jesus, an unschooled and inexperienced "carpenters son" hailing from a tiny fishing village, (Matthew 13:55) time and time again dumbfounding the high and mighty Pharisees and Sadducees from the best religious schools in Jerusalem to Jesus' disciples who were called "men of no schooling that turned the world upside down". (Acts 4:13, Acts 17:6)

From the Apostle Paul, a single man with a "thorn in the flesh" (2 Corinthians 12:7) taking on the greatest scholars of ancient Athens to great men like Martin Luther and John Calvin who centuries after biblical times undermined the entire Roman Catholic, man-centered, works-based system of religion and changed the world because of it; it seems that God Himself has always loved orchestrating a good underdog story! Why has He from the very beginning of the Bible done this time and time and time again?

In first Corinthians chapter 1:27-31 the Apostle Paul tells us why. *"God deliberately chose things the world considers foolish in order to shame those who think they are wise. And he chose those who are powerless to shame those who are powerful. God chose things despised by the world, things counted as nothing at all, and used them to bring to nothing what the world considers important, so that no one can ever boast in the presence of God... As the Scriptures say, "The person who wishes to boast should boast only of what the Lord has done."* The fact of the matter is that often times God loves to do the very thing and use the very people that we would consider "foolish" in order to get the job done because it proves a very important point.

> "Jennie, check yourself for leeches!" I said in disgust. She realized she had two more on her as she looked down and shrieked in dismay. "I don't know if I can do this Scott," she said to me as she sat down on the side of the trail, the weight of her backpack almost toppling her over. I couldn't blame her though, I felt the same way. Even after all the training we had done to get ready for this we were nowhere close to adequate for these trails. Here we were, only a few hours into our first day of hiking and we were already feeling ready to give up. - From page 137 of *Prophecies of Pale Skin*

God takes pleasure in using people that in and of themselves are not fit for the task. People that in and of themselves don't have a whole lot to offer because according to 1 Corinthians, when He does this, man cannot boast about being the one that made the difference by his own measly efforts. He uses the weak things and the foolish people of this world specifically for the purpose of making His glory known!

God knows what He is doing! When we look at ourselves and say "I can't do that because...", "I can't go there because..." or "God can't use me because..." we are undermining the wisdom of God. We are looking at God's agenda laid out for us in scripture through the hazy glasses of the world's wisdom. On the other hand, when we step out in faith in the midst of our fears and inadequacies we are taking God at His word that His grace is sufficient (2 Corinthians 12:9). That He really does know what He is doing in asking us to be His messengers to the last unreached people groups.

> I knew from the moment that we saw the vine bridge that this would be no easy task for Jennie. One of the first things out of her mouth when she herself saw the dangling vines was "Oh man Scott, I'm afraid of heights". If she was going to get across that bridge, something would have to drive her that was greater than her fear of heights and falling. She would have to set her eyes on the other side and step by step, move forward by faith. I will never forget watching her cross the jungle vine bridge that day. The determination on her face, the emotions running through my chest as I watched my young, wife, barely out of her teens climb up on the vines and utter her "last words" just in case the bridge didn't hold. As she began to inch her way across those vines one little sidestep at a time, it became a reality to me that... It was God that was in control, and He would do with her as He saw fit. All I could do was yell words of affirmation and encouragement from the side of the river and watch her step out in faith. - From page 140 of *Prophecies of Pale Skin*

Rest assured that there will always be those on the sidelines, Christian or not, that point and stare and call us fools for what we are doing, but that is always the way it has been even since the days of Moses the "slow of speech" and David "the shepherd boy"! And this is the way it always will be until God Himself finally does away with the wisdom of this world altogether.

> We could see them still clenching their bows and arrows and holding them close. "What are they talking about? Why aren't they putting down their bows and arrows? What will they do next?" I wondered out loud as I looked over at Jennie sitting in the boat right behind me. At that range we couldn't have gotten away from them in time to not be shot even if we had wanted too. They were probably only thirty feet or so away... I can only imagine what must have been going through the minds of the Burate people on the other side of the river as they watched all of this take place from a safe distance. They must have thought we were crazy for getting anywhere close to such people. But then again, there were many of our friends and relatives back in the United States that felt the same way. We knew many people in our homeland that felt as if risks like these should not be taken and that people such as these are not worth such a price. It seemed to be the same on this side of the world. - From page 130 of *Prophecies of Pale Skin*

The wisdom of the world says, "Don't take the risks! You are insufficient for a job like that! It is not worth it!" The wisdom of our King says, "Take the risks! My grace is sufficient! It will be well worth it!" The real question is who's wisdom will we choose to live by and be ruled by - God's wisdom or man's wisdom? Do you really trust that God truly does know what He is doing in giving someone like you the command to "go"?

> I watched Jennie as she picked up one of the children and held it in her arms, cuddling it on her lap as if it were her own. With mud smudges on her beautiful face and little bits of ash and thatch grass hanging from her long, curly yellow hair, she sat there in the middle of the small crowd of Dao women and children and laughed. In that moment as I watched my young wife and best friend sitting in that little thatched roof house, a sense of pride hit me. In the midst of all the negative comments that had been made about her coming on this survey, in spite of all the odds that were stacked against her, she had made it. She had been waiting for this experience for years. These women of this tribe had perhaps been waiting for this for centuries.
> - From page 152 of *Prophecies of Pale Skin*

Questions

1. What are some of your own favorite stories from the Bible or from your own life that are good examples of God doing extraordinary things with insufficient and ordinary people?

2. What are some of the inadequacies and weaknesses in your own life that you often look at through the lenses of "the wisdom of this world" and use as excuses to not serve God?

3. Does your attitude towards your own inadequacies show that you truly believe that God knows what He is doing and that He has a specific agenda for showing His glory through those inadequacies?

4. Who's wisdom are you presently choosing to live by and be ruled by - God's wisdom or man's wisdom? Do you really trust that God knows what He is doing in giving someone like you the command to "go"?

* Read **Exodus 4:10-15** and ponder these verses and how they relate to your own life

DAY

7

WHAT IF
it WAS
YOU?

"With You is the fountain of life;
In your light do we see light."

Psalm 36:9

Day 7: What If It Was You?

Imagine for a moment what life would be like if you were blind. You have been blind from birth. You can hear things like the deep guttural sounds of thunder rumbling across the sky and the powerful crack of lightning strike the treetops around you during a storm but have no idea what these powerful things look like. All you know is that when they come, they scare you to death!

Naturally, in your fear that these incredibly loud rumbles and cracks could harm you, you might ask someone to your right or left to explain what these things are and what they look like. But what if everyone to your right and left was also blind? What if you had not ever known or even met someone that wasn't also blind? In fact, what if no one in your entire community had ever even met someone that could see? Everyone you know and everyone they know were all blind from birth and are also scared spitless of these regularly reoccurring rumbles of thunder and cracks of lightning.

Though you hear these powerful sounds and know they exist, there is literally not a single way that you can see or understand them. In the book of Jonah, as Jonah is sitting on the sidelines of the city, pouting that his source of shade and comfort has been taken from him, God describes the spiritual blindness of the people of Nineveh in a similar way; *"Shouldn't I feel sorry for this important city, Nineveh? It has more than 120,000 people in it as well as many animals. These people couldn't tell their right hand from their left"* He says. (Jonah 4:11)

"Aa too otoogiyoo!" one of the men yelled frantically as he ran circles. We hurried towards the clearing in the middle of the small thatch roofed houses in case one of those huge prehistoric trees was to come crashing down on us. They continued hooting and hollering making their "Whoop! Whoop!" noises as they ran in circles and stomped until the earthquake one again subsided. "What is going on? Why do they run circles and whoop like that? Is it because they are scared?" I asked our Dani guide. "They think there is a giant snake...That is what they think causes the earthquakes: a giant snake with a body the size of a tree trunk. It is said to be a demon snake that goes around underneath the ground causing everything to move and jolt as it slithers along under the surface. That is why they run in circles hollering and stomping! They are trying to get the snake to go away!" he continued. - From page 158 of *Prophecies of Pale Skin*

None of us chose where we were born. You didn't choose to be born in America or Europe or wherever it is that you come from instead of in a staunch Muslim country or in the deepest, darkest, most remote of jungles. The fact that you were not born in a similar state to the Ninevites or the Dao people or any other spiritually dark place where there is not a single person that can *"tell their right hand from their left"* is a gift from God. If you were born in a place with access to the truth then that was the merciful and undeserved act of a gracious God that cares for you. There was not a single thing you did during your pre-existence to deserve it.

> The Dao link earthquakes and unusual natural phenomena with significant events and omens. To them, the fact that these huge earthquakes were taking place during our arrival to their territory was no mere coincidence...The earthquakes came again and again over the following few days until we eventually lost count as to how many had taken place...To top it all off, that very afternoon a huge tropical storm settled in. The clouds let loose and a torrential downpour, unmatched by any I had seen, fell down on us with fury. The lighting strobes continually froze our movements in flashes of white as we sat in the little leak filled thatched roof house waiting out the storm. The deafening cracks of lightning struck up and down the mountain tops all around us and the deep guttural sounds of thunder rumbled across the sky all night. - From page 158 of *Prophecies of Pale Skin*

We can see God's attitude towards people like this, through His pursuing of the Ninevites in Jonah's day. *"Should I not feel compassion for these people?"* God asks. He pursues them and sends a messenger to them even though the messenger himself tries to high tail it the other direction because he wants nothing to do with people like this and has no desire to be a part of what God is doing to bring these people to Himself! *"For God so loved the world...."* John 3:16 cries out to us! THE WORLD! He wants them to know Him and He has an intricate plan to bring every last sheep into the flock.

> Most of the Dao people and especially the children had a lot of soot and dirt caked on their faces from not bathing but this was again a part of their complex belief system. They had reasons for everything that they did. We would continually find out that their social and cultural structure was just as intricate as ours even if it was fairly hard for us to understand. - From page 161 of *Prophecies of Pale Skin*

It is anything but easy to get to unreached people like these. There is a reason why the last remaining untouched people groups of this world, that have not a single shred of the Bible available to them, live in such incredibly hard to reach places. Often times there is a reason the Bible hasn't yet been translated into their languages!

> The Dao language was tonal. It almost sounded like they were singing when they said certain groups of words together. For instance, if they were talking about the cannibalistic tribes in the lowlands and said the sentence "That person eats people" they would say in the Dao language *"Mee mée mee mée nugi"*. We would find out later that three of the four of these *"mee"* words had different meaning according to the context and also the pitch at which you spoke them. This would not by any means be an easy language to learn! It was possibly the only language of the eight hundred plus languages on the island with both tone and accent. We found out later that there were close to twenty different distinct forms of even just the word "go". - From page 161 of *Prophecies of Pale Skin*

But God will not stop compassionately pursuing people like these until every last *"tongue, tribe, people and nation"* has *"representatives standing before the throne and singing His praises"* (Revelation 5:9) and we, as His people and His ambassadors to this world should not stop pursuing and seeking them out either.

> "We are here to bring you a message" we said at first as our Dani guide began to translate. The old chief got quiet and looked at us with interest. "We are from a land very far away but we have hiked into your territory because we want to tell you a story about the Creator of all things" we continued. At this point all the other Dao people in the room were also completely silent. You could have heard a pin drop if it wasn't for the crackling and popping of the fire. "We don't come to bring you material wealth or things of this earth. We come with a message about the trail to eternal life. We come with a message primarily for your spirit" our Dani friend continued to translate as we spoke one phrase at a time. "We want to tell you of these things and give you this important message that we carry but in order to do so we must first learn your language so that we can tell you well in a way that you will understand. In order to do that we would need to move here and live among your people. We would need to spend time learning your language and your ways," we continued and then waited again as the Dani continued translating. - From page 172 of *Prophecies of Pale Skin*

So what if it was you that was born blind? What if there was no one you could turn to in your entire community or city that even had the ability to see the truth? What if you lived day in and day out with the questions that these people live with and had not a single avenue by which you could finally get some answers? You would want someone to come to you wouldn't you?

> The old chief's demeanor had completely changed from earlier. He had a penetrating and serious look in his eyes as he listened. Then a huge hopeful smile swept over his face. He began speaking in his language fast and excited and our guide tried his best to translate as Totopwi spoke..."We have been waiting for your message. Come! We want you to come and live among us! You can have trees for your houses and land to build them on. Come here and live among us and we will help you learn our language. We will help you so that we can hear your message. Thank you! Thank you! Yes, come!" he excitedly replied as the other Dao people in the room also nodded in agreement... We could have jumped up and shouted for joy at hearing the words of that old nearly toothless chief. It seemed God had prepared these people before we had ever hiked into their territory. We hadn't hiked all this way in vain. They wanted us to come. They wanted us to live among them and learn their language. They wanted us to bring them the greatest message of all time. They wanted to learn about their Creator! - From page 173 of *Prophecies of Pale Skin*

Questions

1. Stop and think for a moment about what life would be like if you had never even heard a single verse of scripture. If you had been born in a place without access to the truth or if the Bible you have had never been translated into English. What if you had no way of reading or knowing the words of those pages? How would that affect your daily life?

2. Imagine for a moment how things would be different if you had not a single friend or family member that knew anything about the God of the Bible or that had ever even once heard the name "Jesus". How would this affect your daily hopes and fears?

3. What can we see reflected in the character of our God through His compassionate pursuing of a people like the Ninevites and other unreached people groups?

4. What are some of the things we can learn from Jonah's own outlook of Nineveh, his reaction to God telling him to "go", and his complaints about his lack of comfort once he got there?

5. How can we take active steps to begin searching for and reaching out to those that reside in places without access to a single shred of the truth available to them in their language and culture? What can we do to start proactively being a part of seeing these people have their first opportunity to hear of their Creator's love for them?

* Read **2 Corinthians 4:3-6** and ponder these verses and how they relate to your own life.

DAY

8

Is GOD
a LIAR?

"I saw a vast crowd, too great to count, from every nation and tribe and people and language, standing in front of the throne and before the Lamb. They were clothed in white and held palm branches in their hands. And they were shouting with a mighty shout, "Salvation comes from our God on the throne and from the Lamb!"

Revelation 7:9-10

Day 8: Is God A Liar?

How much is God's reputation worth to Him? If He makes a promise can we count on Him to keep it? Will He be faithful to His own Word no matter what the cost? Hebrews 6:18 tells us *"These two things cannot change: God cannot lie when he makes a promise, and he cannot lie when he makes an oath. These things encourage us who came to God for safety. They give us strength to hold on to the hope we have been given."*

Sometimes, it may feel like there are not many things that we can be sure of and count on in our day and age but one thing we can always count on no matter what the circumstance is that *"God cannot lie"*. And according to this verse this fact should be an encouragement specifically to those that come to God and trust in Him for their safety.

> By the time we were headed down the last mountain, our knees were so weak that they rapidly and involuntarily shook with every downward step... Jennie and I had so many bruises and scrapes on the backs of our legs from slipping and then sliding down various parts of the mountainside that our legs were beginning to resemble raw meat. Our hands and arms swelled out in various places where we had been scraped by jungle thorns and creepers...We could see by the blood stains on our socks and muddy pants that those leeches had sucked way more than their fair share... It couldn't have been clearer that God had given us just enough strength to accomplish our task though we in and of ourselves had felt completely inadequate. He didn't give any more than we needed or any less, He gave us exactly what we needed. And most important of all He had given us favor in the eyes of the Dao people. It would have only taken one man and one of those many bows and arrows we had seen and the survey could have gone bad, not to mention one or all of us could have ended up dead. As I lay there that night drifting in and out of sleep on that hard floor an old saying once again came to mind: "We are immortal until our work is done."- From pages 178-180 of *Prophecies of Pale Skin*

In modern times, it is easy to trust in a hundred other things before we trust God for our peace of mind and safety. Car insurance, home owners insurance, health insurance and good medical care, retirement funds, alarm systems, the self-defense classes I took, the mace keychain on my keys or my gun permit, the local police and firemen or our countries armed forces just to name a few! These are the things that we often times trust in and run to and lean on for peace of mind and safety, not God. But according to Hebrews 6:18 when it comes to our safety, God's commitment to His word and His promises are our ultimate encouragement.

> I rocked back and forth in the bed in the fetal position...I had never experienced a sickness anything like this! Eventually I came to the conclusion that for sure I was going to die. Just the month before we had heard about an American translator a few hours west from us that had contracted cerebral malaria and it had gone into his brain and killed him. He had gone to bed complaining of a headache and the next morning his wife had found him dead. I decided it would be good to say goodbye to Jennie and tell her that I loved her one last time just in case I was headed for the same fate as the missionary we had heard about..."I love you Jennie... If for some reason I don't make it through tonight you keep on going forward okay? Keep on going towards those Dao people and don't give up until they have had their chance to finally hear about their Creator and what He has done for them for the first time alright?" she nodded in agreement as she looked down at her hand in mine and the tears ran down her face. - From page 184 of *Prophecies of Pale Skin*

The fact that God does not lie is not only a great encouragement in relation to the safety of His people but it is also an incredible encouragement in relation to His plan for this world. Why? Because it means that those of us who go out as ambassadors for His name and lay everything on the line for the sake of God's glory and the advancement of His kingdom are living for something that ultimately cannot fail. We are investing our lives in not only a plan but also a promise because God cannot and will not lie.

Isaiah 48:9-11 are some of the many verses in the Bible that show God's commitment to His own glory and to the integrity of His name and reputation. *"For my name's sake I defer my anger, for the sake of my praise I restrain it for you, that I may not cut you off. Behold, I have refined you, but not as silver; I have tried you in the furnace of affliction. For my own sake, for my own sake, I do it, for how should my name be profaned? My glory I will not give to another."*

If God says He is going to do something then He can be trusted to do it. One of the greatest encouragements to us as missionaries and ambassadors of the cross is that we are investing our lives in something that ultimately cannot fail! Because for the sake of His own name, God will not let it fail *"for how should my name be profaned?"* He asks. God will not let Himself be made into a liar! Even if we as the message bearers lose our lives for the sake of the advancement of our message, we lay down our lives for something that will go beyond us and that God will not let end in defeat. The integrity of His name is at stake if He doesn't see it through!

> A couple days before moving into the jungle permanently we took all the rest of our savings that we hadn't spent on food and house building supplies and gave it away. We transferred our savings to a local non-profit organization that had been a huge help to us over the years and left it also behind. We had nothing left. The way we saw it there were no returns and no retreats. This was a one way road and we didn't want anything in our lives that could possibly become an excuse for giving up. To us, giving up the last of our reserves was symbolism, like the cutting of an anchor from a ship: it was the cutting loose of any remaining dead weight that might keep us from running our course well. - From page 186 of *Prophecies of Pale Skin*

No earthly pleasure can be cut loose that will not be worth the loss in the end. God's word to us should be more than just a set of nice stories that we have heard since we were children in Sunday school. And true faith is not merely agreeing that they are nice stories or even that they are true (James 2:19). God's Word is the very reputation and story and character of God Himself played out right in front of us! They are words that can be counted on and words that should be lived by, Words that are to be demonstrated in and throughout our decisions and our lives.

> We purposely decided before we ever started building that we wanted to go as simple as possible in the house building process. This was so that we could model with our lives as well as our words that we were there for only one reason, which was to get them the most important message they would ever hear as quickly as we could get it to them. We felt it was contrary to our message to spend months upon months building nice fancy houses...We wanted our lives to match our message from the beginning. We wanted them to not only hear in our words but more importantly to see in our lives that our message and learning their language so that we could share it with them was the most important thing to us. -From page 190 of *Prophecies of Pale Skin*

There is nothing that better demonstrates that we believe God is true to his Word and reputation and that He *"does not lie"* than when we lay it all on the line for the sake of the advancement of His kingdom, when we rush to the front lines and go to the hard places for the sake of His name and His reputation.

Is there ever a battle where soldiers don't come back bruised and bloody? Is there ever a war where those soldiers on the front lines don't at times long for some relief from their foreign surroundings and dream about the comforts of their homeland? Is there ever a war where some don't make the ultimate sacrifice for their cause?

The isolation from our families and the rest of the world was beginning to take its toll...The beautiful lines of tall jungle trees around our village started to seem less and less beautiful and began to feel a little more like prison bars...The Dao kids that always leaned up next to us and relentlessly petted our arms and tugged on our strange yellow hair didn't seem so cute anymore. In fact, we had both contracted scabies from the village kids and were itching relentlessly... We had been dealing with giardia and amoeba from eating most our meals with them also....After a while, when the people came up to our porch seeking medicine for the stinking, festering slashes on their backs and arms, yellow puss oozing out of them because they refused to bathe, it took everything in us to look on them with compassion anymore...I was tired of being there. The job of learning their language was starting to seem impossible and my patience was wearing thin... "What are we doing here?" I thought to myself as I lay in bed that night. "God, I don't love these people, and I don't think we can learn this language."...I didn't know how much longer we could last out there. Everything inside of me wanted to give up and it was obvious from our past few conversations that Jennie felt the same way. -From pages 201-205 of *Prophecies of Pale Skin*

But on the day that the war is won, and the King declares that the victory is ours, just like He said it would be, the celebration begins! And any sorrow that was faced or any hardship that we endured will be drowned out by the eternal joy of being in the presence of our loving God who not only sent us out, but also empowered us along the way and even orchestrated the victory for the sake of His own great name and reputation.

The bottom line is that when God tells us in His word that at the end of time, there will be "*A vast crowd, too great to count,* ***from every***

nation and tribe and people and language, *standing in front of the throne and before the Lamb. They were clothed in white and held palm branches in their hands. And they were shouting with a mighty shout, "Salvation comes from our God on the throne and from the Lamb!"* (Revelation 7:9-10) those words are as good as gold!

> Looking up at my face and directly into my eyes, Apius continued. "Friend, when I saw you and your wife hike into our valley and I saw your pale skin, and then I saw you building a house here and trying to learn our language, and you told us you had an important message for us, I remembered my father's dream. Upon remembering the dream I decided I would do everything I could to help you learn our language as quickly as possible. I am here, living with you and helping you because I am waiting for the day I can hear your message. That is why I built my house here." I could hardly believe what I was hearing. -From page 205 of *Prophecies of Pale Skin*

There is no people group, no nation, no tribe or language that a missionary can go to in this world without the assured hope of God doing something great. Why? Because if there is even one nation, one tribe, one people or language group missing on that great day when we are all gathered before the throne singing and shouting His praises, then what does that make God? It makes Him a liar! And God is not a liar! And neither will He let Himself be made into one. For the sake of His own name and reputation He will see His plan through to completion for *"How shall my name be profaned? My glory I will not give to another*!"

> As I went in and propped my door open once again for the day's traffic of giggly kids and festering wounds I realized something very important. I understood for the first time that morning that what was going on there in the Dao valley was so much bigger than me. It was about so much more than my wife and I and our measly efforts. This whole thing was not about us at all in fact! God had a plan for these people since long before we ever arrived. Even though they had been forgotten by the rest of the world, God had not forgotten about them... Multiple men had experienced the same prophecy through dreams and passed it on to their children and clan also. God had been giving them these prophetic dreams to prepare them!.. Before we had ever arrived here God's predetermined plan of having "people from every tongue, tribe, people and nation one day standing before his throne" as the Book of Revelation talks about, had been put into play! -From page 206 of *Prophecies of Pale Skin*

I realized that morning that God was even more committed to His Word than I was because if even one of the tribes was missing on that final day when everyone was standing before God's throne, that would make Him a liar. And God is not a liar, nor will He let Himself be made into one!..We realized that we would not fail if we would just let the Lord be the strength that we needed and keep on moving forward....Not because we were anything special or had what it takes to make someone place their faith in Jesus Christ but because God loved these people and was committed to His words. He would not let His purposes fail. We just had to be faithful and speak when God told us to speak. We had to let God be God and let Him do the rest. -From page 207 of *Prophecies of Pale Skin*

Questions

1. Stop and think for a moment what it would be like if we could not trust the fact that "God never lies". What would that mean for you and the way you view God and His word? Why is it so important in our lives as believers that God always keeps His word?

2. What do you put your faith in on a daily basis for your safety? What do you find yourself investing in and counting on and placing your trust in to keep you safe? Are the words of Hebrews 4:16 a reality in your life? Is your ultimate encouragement in relation to your safety in God Himself and His character?

3. What does it mean for missions and every tongue, tribe, people and nation that God has an intense commitment to the integrity of His name as shown in Isaiah 48:9-11?

4. Will missions fail and some tongues, tribes, people and nations never have a chance to hear about their Creator just because we refuse to "go" or get involved? In other words, if God really does have a commitment to His name and His word as shown in the Bible, does the success of God's plan for this world ultimately rest on humanity or on God Himself?

5. Since God has a commitment to His name and will not let His Word be void (Isaiah 55:11) or His plans fail, who is it that ultimately misses out if we refuse to get involved with what He has commanded us to be a part of? Does God miss out or is it ultimately us that misses out on the privilege of playing a part?

* Read **Psalm 67** and ponder these verses and how they relate to your own life.

DAY

9

CULTURE
or CHRIST;
WHICH ONE
is KING?

"When I am with the Gentiles...
I fit in with them as much as I can.
In this way, I gain their confidence
and bring them to Christ...Yes, I try to
find common ground with everyone
so that I might bring them to Christ.
I do all this to spread the Good News,
and in doing so I enjoy its blessings."

1 Corinthians 9:20-23

Day 9: Culture Or Christ; Which One Is King?

Have you ever stopped and thought about what Jesus embraced in order to minister to us?

Before He came down to the earth and subjected Himself to the confines of humanity He had not yet taken on the burdens of the human body. Jesus had no need for clothes because He was spirit. Perhaps He had never felt physical hunger or thirst. He had no need for food because He was not dependent on daily nutrition to live. He had never experienced a splinter in His hand from a rough piece of wood in the carpentry shop, a stomach bug that sent Him bolting to the bathroom nor eaten a bad piece of fish that sent Him running from the kitchen table to empty His stomach all over the floor. And worst of all, He had never experienced a crown of thorns being pounded down onto His skull and having His body pierced, tortured and crucified for the sake of the ones that He loved. (Hebrews 2:14-18)

Now, for all eternity He still remains in that scarred body which serves as a standing testament to His love, He still bears the marks on His body from when He was pierced (John 20:27), even though for eternity past He had existed without its confines. What an incredible love He has, that He was willing to alter His state for all eternity for us. Truly, "*There is no greater love than this. That a man would lay down his life for his friends.*" (John 15:13)

When He came to us, although He could have done so, He didn't choose an extra strong and muscle bound perfect body like many of us might have if we were in His position. In fact, Isaiah 53 says *"There was nothing beautiful or majestic about his appearance, nothing to attract us to him"*. He chose to identify with us for one purpose and with only one goal in mind. He chose to be "*despised and rejected, a man of sorrows, acquainted with bitterest grief.*" And humanities reaction to Him was this: "*we turned our backs on him and looked the other way when he went by. He was despised, and we did not care. Yet it was our weaknesses he carried; it was our sorrows that weighed him down. And we thought his troubles were a punishment from God for his own sins! But he was*

72

wounded and crushed for our sins. He was beaten that we might have peace. He was whipped, and we were healed!" (Isaiah 53:2-5)

"Do you pale skinned people die?" Daokagi again asked me with a very serious look on his face. "Well yes, of course we die"…"Friend, I am afraid to die. What will happen to my spirit? Will it go to the place of demons to become an evil spirit as our ancestors told us it will? What will happen to me? I do not know. I am very afraid of death," he continued and then looked at me with such a hopeless look on his face as if he didn't know what to do with himself. "When you tell us the words from the Creator's leaf book, will you tell us of these things?" he asked. "Yes friend, we will tell you of these things" I nodded in agreement… A grim smile stretched across his face. "I hope I live long enough to hear this message. I am so afraid of death," he said. Then he got up and slowly walked back down the jungle trail to his own house.
-From page 211 of *Prophecies of Pale Skin*

There is a good reason that the New Testament makes it a point to tell us to *"arm yourselves with the same attitude he had"* (1 Peter 4:1). Jesus wants us to make it a point to try to identify with those that we are ministering to in the same way that He Himself identified with us. The Apostle Paul was so convinced of this truth that he tells us he even took it as far as to *"become like"* the Jews while he was ministering to the Jews and to become like the Gentiles while he was ministering to the Gentiles. Paul said *"I fit in with them as much as I can in order to gain their confidence and bring them to Christ"* as long as it did not put him in a position in which he had to *"discard the law of God"* or to not *"obey the law of Christ"*. (1 Corinthians 9:20-23)

This is the opposite of what I saw growing up in church circles. I saw people that had formed their own "Christian culture" and values, which dictated everything from clothes style to what one could eat or drink or smoke. There was an entire set of rules and stipulations unsupported by scripture but ruthlessly enforced both in and outside the church. It was a system completely separate from the words of the Bible that was in and of itself a sort of social control. A man-made set of rules, which struck fear into the church members and ultimately decided who would and wouldn't be labeled a true Christian.

This way of thinking was one that wanted nothing to do with, as the Apostle Paul put it, *"fitting in with"* the cultures and sub-cultures of the unbelievers we are trying to minister to *"in order to gain their confidence and bring them to Christ"*.

I along with the people I spent Sundays with growing up were so fearful of the judgments of the church culture itself that most were afraid to carry out the example of this man that we claimed to follow - Jesus.

> Yakiyaa was unusually quiet that evening so I could tell that there was something on his mind... He looked at me for a second across the fire and then held out the cigarette in front of him, pointing it towards me. "We heard recently that there is another man that is claiming to have the message of the Creator. He is teaching in the next tribe over but they say that he is from the Dani tribe many weeks walk from here. We have heard that he teaches there is a place of fire that the enemies of the Creator One will go to. The man says that if we smoke tobacco and wear our decorative nosebones, if we carry our bows and arrows and wear our traditional dress, if we do not leave our ways behind and begin to wear the strange clothes of you pale skinned foreigners, we will go to this place of fire. Is this true? Does the Creator One that you have come to tell us about hate the way we look and the ways of our people? Will He send me to His place of fire because of this tobacco that I am smoking?" he somberly asked. -From page 217 of *Prophecies of Pale Skin*

Most of those I attended church with were so busy playing the part and so afraid of looking unspiritual or offending the men and women that were leading the way and enforcing this "Christian culture" that we lost our passion for doing anything great all together. The highest form of our Christian activity was to simply never offend anyone within the church, everything else became secondary, including Jesus Christ.

To my surprise, when I traveled overseas I quickly found that in the few cities of Indonesia that had been missionized and where there had been church buildings built, once again, this type of view was dominating many of the churches in these places as well. Men that usually wore the traditional dress of their people and carried bows and arrows during the week, would magically appear at the church building on Sunday in a clean, button up, white collared shirt, complete with dress pants and a tie to match. The bow and arrows they always kept by their side and traditional dress they were wearing just the day before would be nowhere in sight and they would walk around with their chests puffed out in pride sporting the western clothes that had presumably been provided to them recently by the missionaries.

Why do we humans so quickly latch on to things like this? Why is it that anywhere in the world that the message of Jesus is preached, whether its in high-tech modern cities or small remote villages on the edge of the jungle, this seems to be one of the first tactics that Satan uses to try to confuse the young community of believers?

> "I reached across the room and grabbed the cigarette out of Yakiyaa's hand. I wanted so bad to show him that I didn't believe these lies they had been told by other tribes anymore than they should. I put the cigarette up to my lips and took a big puff. Nearly gagging on the smoke I began uncontrollably coughing, as I had never smoked a cigarette in my entire life. I exhaled and watched the smoke twirl up to the top of the room as Yakiyaa's eyes widened and he looked across the room with his jaw hanging wide open in shock. "Well if this is what sends a person to the place of hellfire, I guess I am going there too since I also have now smoked some of your tobacco!" I said while looking him directly in the eyes. "But this is not the message that we bring Yakiyaa. The message that the Dani you have heard about is carrying around is a lie straight from the evil spirits themselves! It is not the message from the Creator's leaf book that saves someone from the place of fire! When we have learned your language well enough I will open up the leaf book of the Creator One. With your own eyes you will have the opportunity to see what the Creator One has to say about it. You and your people will finally hear about the one and only true trail to eternal life."- From pages 218-219 of *Prophecies of Pale Skin*

Satan knows our weaknesses. He knows that our human pride in ourselves and what we do to look good in front of others is one of the most effective tools he can use against the true Jesus-magnifying, cross-cherishing, self-denying message of the gospel.

Satan is no fool and he has been using this trick against the spread of a passion for the glory of God alone ever since the days of Adam and Eve in the garden of Eden, when they in their foolish pride thought they knew better than their Creator Himself. This is not a new strategy from the enemy of God. Satan has been using it for centuries to wreak havoc among God's people and to draw people away from God's loving plan for them.

One of the most cunning strategies of this deceiver Satan which he comes back to and uses against us time and time again is to simply get us to believe that we know better. If he can get us to replace the God-saturated foundation of Scripture for why we do what we do with our own man-made premise for what is and isn't good, then the battle is over and he has succeeded.

> I again reflected on my childhood and many of the lies I had heard growing up and been taught in "Christian" schools and churches. We made a decision that night that God's book would be our standard for what is right and what is wrong, not the church culture we had been raised in or the opinions of men that had been pushed on us and had distorted the truth in our own lives for so long...Through both our words and through our lives we wanted the Dao people to know true good news and nothing else. - From page 219 of *Prophecies of Pale Skin*

This tyrant called "Christian culture" that dominates and sits on the throne of many churches today both in the USA and as far away as the small cities of Papua, Indonesia, this shallow substitute, this decoy which is held up in place of the Bible as our authority for what is right and wrong, is one of the greatest enemies to the advancement of the pure, unadulterated cross-centered gospel of the true King.

Questions

1. What are some different ways that "arming ourselves with the same attitude Jesus had" (1 Peter 4:1) will dynamically affect our lives both in the realm of our responses to suffering and also in our attitude towards ministering to lost people of different cultures and subcultures both in our own country and abroad?

2. Do you think it is as important for us in our day to try to *"become like"* the people we are trying to minister to *"in order to gain their confidence and bring them to Christ"* as it was for the Apostle Paul?

3. What should be our standard for how far we are willing to take the whole concept of *"fitting in"* and *"becoming like"* the people we are trying to minister to? What did Paul say he made the boundary for how far he was willing to go with this concept? (1 Corinthians 9:21)

4. What did Paul say was his ultimate standard for what is and isn't acceptable for the Christian to do in order to bring others to Christ? (1 Corinthians 9:21) Should this also be our standard?

5. When the Pharisees elevated their own spiritual culture and extra-biblical rules and laws above even the teachings and words of Jesus Himself, what was Jesus' reaction to them? What was Jesus reaction to their trying to enforce their "super-spiritual" culture on Him and His disciples? What did Jesus call them? (Matthew 15:7-9)

* Read **Matthew 15:1-20** and ponder these verses and how they relate to your own life.

DAY

10

HAVE WE SETTLED *for* *a* SUBSTITUTE?

"Yes, they knew God, but they wouldn't worship him as God or even give him thanks. And they began to think up foolish ideas of what God was like. The result was that their minds became dark and confused. Claiming to be wise, they became utter fools instead. And instead of worshiping the glorious, ever-living God, they worshiped idols made to look like mere people, or birds and animals and snakes."

Romans 1:21-23

Day 10: Have We Settled For A Substitute?

What happens when a sure foundation has been replaced with a shallow substitute?

There was a time when the whole world, every living human being knew the story of God. They knew that He was the highest Authority, the Creator. They knew that He was the most powerful Being in the universe and that He has an ultimate claim on us as His creations. They knew that life exists because of Him and that no life could have existed without Him.

They even knew the story of their first ancestors Adam and Eve and the story of the deception of the great serpent and its affect on mankind. They knew about the sons of Adam and Eve and why the very first murder in the history of humankind had occurred. These words, the words of God that are recorded in Genesis, were common knowledge. There wasn't a person on earth that did not know these stories!

So what happened? Romans chapter 1:21-25 makes it pretty clear; *"Yes, they knew God, but they wouldn't worship him as God or even give him thanks. And they began to think up foolish ideas of what God was like. The result was that their minds became dark and confused. Claiming to be wise, they became utter fools instead. And instead of worshiping the glorious, ever-living God, they worshiped idols made to look like mere people, or birds and animals and snakes."*

"Degapiyaa, no! Don't go back out there yet!...Those colors, they are the walking stick of the evil spirits. They are a bad omen, do not look at them! They could cause you sickness or even death!" Wikipai replied... they really did believe that this is what a rainbow was, the literal walking stick of an evil spirit! We couldn't believe that they were so afraid of something so beautiful. Something that, according to the message we wanted to bring them, had been given as a sign of goodwill and of a promise from God to Noah and all of mankind. In the Dao culture, this sign of goodwill from God had been turned into a sign of the evil spirits, something that they believed could cause them harm and which was meant to bring sickness and even death. - From page 229 of *Prophecies of Pale Skin*

The first step in any society on this earth towards that society's ultimate spiritual demise is their making the mistake of believing that they know better than God. It does not matter what we replace our Creator and His story with, whether we try to replace God with our own system of rights and wrongs or try to deny God's existence altogether, if we replace His ultimate claim and authority over us as His creation, then we have taken the first step towards our own destruction. This is what has happened to cultures and people groups around the world from the most primitive man in the jungles to the most advanced society in Europe. From one place to another around the globe the result has been the same over and over again.

Paul saw it in his day and we see it in ours as well; *"They think up foolish ideas of what God is like...their minds become dark and confused. Claiming to be wise, they become utter fools instead. Instead of worshiping the ever-living God, they worship idols...they do vile and degrading things with each other's bodies...they deliberately choose to believe lies. They worship the things God made but not the Creator himself. Even the women turn against the natural way to have sex and instead indulge in sex with each other. And the men, instead of having normal sexual relationships with women, burn with lust for each other. Men do shameful things with other men and, as a result, suffer within themselves the penalty they so richly deserve...Their lives are full of every kind of wickedness, sin, greed, hate, envy, murder, fighting, deception, malicious behavior, and gossip. They are backstabbers, haters of God, insolent, proud, and boastful. They are forever inventing new ways of sinning..."* (verses 21-32).

"Was it Jennie's friend Etokaatadi they were talking about? Surely they hadn't killed her!" I wondered as my heartbeat quickened and I looked around for someone else to ask for an explanation...Then it hit me, Daokagi was in on it too! He had always treated Etokaatadi as if he would have been happier if she were dead. This murder had been planned from the very start and it was Etokaatadi's very husband that had probably instigated it! We found out the rest of the details as the day went on. Daokagi had falsely blamed his wife Etokaatadi for causing two other recent deaths through witchcraft. Daapoi knew what he had to do. He knew it was his responsibility being the younger brother of Daokagi to avenge these two deaths. There was no other way. He had to do it. He had to kill Etokaatadi for the witchcraft she had supposedly worked on these two men. This was what their animistic beliefs demanded of them. - From page 231 of *Prophecies of Pale Skin*

Could there be a better description of the materialistic, money-centered, sex-worshipping, God-barren type of behavior that we see today even in our own society than what we read in Romans 1?

Whether it is a man-made system of Christian culture that we elevate above God and His word to us or whether it is some other idol or system of belief that we hold up in His place, the end result is a twisted and godless society. A society that goes from one hollow thing to another just trying to suck a little bit more physical pleasure out of a dry, sand-filled cistern that can't even compare to the cold clear spring that is Jesus Himself. In the words of the prophet Jeremiah, we have become people that *"...have done two evil things: They have forsaken me - the fountain of living water. And they have dug for themselves cracked cisterns that can hold no water at all!"* (Jeremiah 2:13)

Every person, culture and people group that exists in this world had the truth at one time, we don't have to look much further than the legends and folk stories of any people group to see evidence that this is the case. And we don't have to look any further than their actions to see the hopelessness, murder and sin that results in forsaking the words of life and instead sucking on old, dry, *"cracked cisterns that can hold no water at all"*.

Wikipai continued on (telling me the Dao peoples beliefs surrounding the creation of mankind and the first Dao people on earth) "Because the older brother had not been patient and had used the wrong type of leaves, some of the blood from the corpse dripped down into the ground next to that special tree which was next to that river. When it dripped down into the ground it seeped right into the mouth of a great evil spirit snake. For this very reason, even to this day we Dao people die. It is said that if there had not been that disagreement between the two brothers and that blood had not gone into the great serpent's mouth next to that special tree, we would live forever!" Wikipai explained. This story sounded strangely familiar! A disagreement between two brothers? A special tree? A serpent that was responsible for the death of all mankind? It sounded like a very skewed version of the Bible's Genesis account and some of the events surrounding the Biblical account of the creation of mankind! This surely was strange! This wasn't the only story they told us that had similarities to some of the stories told in the Old Testament. - From page 235 of *Prophecies of Pale Skin*

So when one chooses to turn from the cracked dry cisterns that our own foolish pride has to offer and instead turns and runs to the cool, fresh, pure, clean water that is Jesus, what is the result? This Oasis that they find in the desert, this Water in a dry and barren land becomes the center of their attention, the very focal point of their entire life! They just can't seem to get enough of that sweet, cool refreshing Water that is God Himself. In their joy at finding this wonderful Spring of life giving water they begin commending it to others, they just can't stop talking about this rare treasure that has changed their life completely.

"Why don't you just go back to the States for now and recuperate. The Dao people aren't going anywhere! They will still be in the jungle when you get back!" they would urge...Perhaps the other missionaries were right, maybe we should go back to America...just for a little while? We could never bring ourselves to take this advice though. It didn't sit right with our conscience. It seemed like we were getting more reports of new deaths every other week. How could we look the Dao people in the eyes and tell them "Once we learn your language well enough we will tell you the most important message that you will ever hear." but then take a vacation and take it easy for a while, in turn making it a longer period of time before they heard our "important message"?... "What does this say about our message when we don't even care enough to endure through hardship so that people can hear it!... It says that Jesus isn't worth it to us, doesn't it? It says that our comforts and health and families and American foods are worth more than the our message doesn't it?"...We couldn't just speak about our message as if it were important to us, we had to live it... We couldn't rest until our Dao friends had a chance to hear about Jesus and His trail to eternal life for the first time. They were hopeless without it. - From pages 242-243 of *Prophecies of Pale Skin*

If we truly have experienced Jesus, if God Himself truly has become our greatest Treasure and our Source of spiritual life and He is the Center of our universe, then the exact opposite will happen to us from what Paul explains has happened to those in Romans 1. "We will know God and worship Him as God and give Him thanks. We will leave behind our foolish ideas of what He is like and the result will be that our minds become clear and vibrant. We will claim ourselves to be fools in comparison to the all knowing, all-powerful God that we worship! And we will turn from the foolish idols we have replaced our Creator with and turn back to our source of hope and true life that is God Himself."

We will see Jesus for who He truly is and as a result be willing not only to turn from any lesser joy or idol and live for Him, but for the sake of making known the treasure that He can be to others, we will even be willing to forsake everything else for Him. We will go to great lengths to encourage others also to turn back to the sure foundation that they have traded in for a shallow substitute.

Questions

1. What is your foundation for life? If you know God Himself as the highest Authority and believe that He as your Creator has an ultimate claim on you then is this being reflected in your life and demonstrated in your daily decisions?

2. Do you think your own society as a whole, being a place that has a general knowledge of God and multiple avenues by which it can have access to God's Word, is turning more and more towards God or more and more away from Him?

3. Why is it important to guard God's Word as our only ultimate standard? If our society is presently turning more and more away from God as our sure foundation, according to Romans 1:21-32, what will be the end result? What type of things will take place in our families and the generations of our children and grandchildren?

4. What are some of the dry and cracked cisterns that repeatedly threaten the wellbeing of my own family and life? What are some of the shallow substitutes that compete for the place of the cool clean refreshing water that is Jesus alone?

5. Does my life reflect to the people I am trying to minister to that Jesus alone is the ultimate Treasure? Am I holding Him up and commending Him as my supreme Pleasure and Source of refreshment in this dry and barren land?

* Read **Matthew 13:44-48** and ponder these verses and how they relate to your own life.

DAY

11

WHAT *is it that* WE CANNOT DO?

*"The thief's purpose is to steal
and kill and destroy.
My purpose is to give life
in all its fullness."*

John 10:10

Day 11: What Is It That We Cannot Do?

Where do the shallow substitutes, the dry, sand-filled cisterns that Satan tries to get us to turn to and suck on over and over again lead? What is he trying to accomplish by getting us to turn away from the cool, clear, satisfying Spring that is only found in God Himself? (Jeremiah 2:13)

According to John 10:10 *"The thief's purpose is to steal and kill and destroy."* That is what Satan desires for us. That is what his end goal is in trying to turn us to lesser joys and decoys and in trying to get us to lay our lives on a shallow substitute instead of on the sure foundation that is God Himself. He desires our eternal destruction.

> Apiyaawogi's wife, Wadamenaa grabbed a sharp piece of bamboo with one hand while she pinched and puffed up a big tuft of skin on Paatoma's ankle with the other hand. In a quick sawing like motion she sliced him multiple times as another man, Uwokaatomaa grabbed a thick decorative arrow with a human killing tip and pulled it back on his bow string. Jennie turned her head as the blood spurted out of Paatoma's ankle, even I felt nauseous when I saw things like this. Pointing his bow up toward the sky he released the arrow... As the arrow shot through the air he yelled a final "Go now you evil spirits! Bother Paatoma no longer!" The blood from Paatoma's ankle and foot dripped down into the ground for nearly an hour. When it had finally stopped dripping they dug up the dirt where his blood had spread down into the ground and threw it in the fire just in case it might attract evil spirits to the place where they had performed the spirit chasing ceremony...We had for the first time begun to understand why the Dao people have so many scars all over their bodies, why they constantly have wounds that are infected and we had to spend so much time cleaning out infected, oozing gashes day after day: this was their traditional medicine. This was their belief system. - From pages 246-247 of *Prophecies of Pale Skin*

What is Jesus' goal? Again in John 10:10 Jesus states *"My purpose is to give life in all its fullness"*. That is what Jesus desires for us in pointing us towards His Father, towards God Himself. He is what Jesus gives us access to through His death on the cross on our behalf. That is what His end goal is in getting us to turn away from the dry broken cisterns that we replace Him with...He wants to give us *"life in all its fullness"*!

When we take up the cause of Jesus in this world and seek to be a part of making Him known we are doing nothing less than pointing to "*life in all its fullness*". We are spending our time and lives drinking from and rejoicing in and pointing others to the "*water of life*" (John 4:10) For us as mere ambassadors and message bearers however there is something we cannot do in this whole endeavor.

"The evil spirits want us to die so that they can feast on our bodies. We will become their food. Our loved ones will wrap us in our bark rain capes and place us in the trees when we die and the evil spirits will feast on our bodies until we are no more. They are all evil. There is not a single spirit that is good. Curse them all!" Paatoma told us. For days Jennie and I talked through and hashed over what we heard that day from Paatoma. "Cannibal spirits! Can you believe it Jennie? How are we supposed to convey to the Dao people that God the Creator is spirit and that He is good when the only spirits they have ever known are evil and want to do them harm?" We had come to the realization that the message we travelled all the way from the other side of the world to tell them about was in many ways the exact opposite of everything they had ever known and believed...Unless God opened up their eyes and did what we as mere message bearers could never ourselves do, our being there and our leaving behind everything that we had ever known was in vain. - From page 249 of *Prophecies of Pale Skin*

Perhaps you have heard the old saying, "You can lead a horse to water but you can't make it drink". To many people, those old, dry, sand-filled cisterns are all they have ever known and the refreshing water of life in the middle of the dessert looks about like a small child sees a big plate of spinach.

There is something that has to occur in the mind and eyes of the individual that is used to sucking on sand and substitutes in the dessert before he will bend down on his knees, cup his hands, and take that first, sweet, life-giving drink. A desire has to form in his heart to taste what is lying before him. A thirst has to exist for something that he has never tasted or known before. As Jesus said to the Samaritan women, "*If you only knew the gift God has for you and who I am, you would ask me, and I would give you living water.*" (John 4:10)

"You have always told us that when you knew our language well you would tell us of the message from the Creator's leaf book. The words that will show us the trail to eternal life! You speak well enough now, don't you?...Will it be soon?" Wikipai asked with an inquisitive look in his eyes. He was right...and we were continuing to get reports almost weekly of more Dao men and women dying through revenge killings, tribal warfare, homicide and sickness. "How many more of the Dao people will die before they have even had their first chance to hear about their Creator and what He has done to provide them with eternal life?" I thought as I looked Wikipai in the eyes...That was the day that we finally knew it was time. God wasn't working in only us now. Despite our doubts and despite how incredibly daunting the task seemed of explaining such deep Biblical concepts to such an animistic, remote group of people, it was obvious that God was also already working in the Dao people and beginning to draw them to Himself. He was preparing them for His message and many of them were waiting for His words! It seemed His message was irresistible to Wikipai. As if it called to him like a long lost treasure that he had been waiting for and dreaming of. - From pages 250-251 of *Prophecies of Pale Skin*

It doesn't matter what missionaries leave behind. It doesn't matter what hardships we may have gone through to get to the people far back in the middle of the jungles and unreached Muslim countries of the world. It doesn't matter whether we have spent two years or twenty years learning an extremely hard language in hopes of giving these people the gospel. It even doesn't matter if we have impeccable methodology and tell the story of the Bible in a clear, complete and dynamic fashion in which it has never been taught before!

We can leave everything behind and travel across the world and preach until we are blue in the face and have nothing left to give, but if God does not do what we cannot do as mere message bearers there will be no true and lasting change in the hearts of our listeners. God Himself has to do a miracle that only He can do. He has to create a thirst in our listeners that will cause them to not only see the living water from afar, but also to actually walk to the water's edge, get down on their knees and begin lapping up that sweet, refreshing water that is Jesus.

As we talked through the beliefs and culture of the Dao people we came to the conclusion that we could not just start translating and teaching in the New Testament with the life of Christ. These were animistic people and they believed that there were literally hundreds of spirits that infiltrated everything and every aspect of life. According to the Dao belief system, every single one of the spirits was evil and ultimately sought to do them harm. They had no concept of one great Creator spirit that was good in nature, more powerful than all others and ultimately sovereign over all things, both good and evil...We had to lay a correct foundation and begin teaching from the Creation account in the book of Genesis. We had to lay a solid foundation for the understanding of God's character through the Old Testament stories or the Dao people might end up even worse off than before. If we did not start from Genesis and the concept of one good Creator God over all things, then the Dao tribe would likely just turn into a group of people that sought to appease the American "Jesus Spirit" along with all the other spirits. - From page 253 of *Prophecies of Pale Skin*

Only two chapters after His words to the Samaritan women in the book of John, Jesus continues on saying, *"Everyone **whom my Father gives** me will come to me. I will never turn away anyone who comes to me"* (John 6:37) and then in John 6:44 he says; *"**People cannot come** to me **unless the Father who sent me draws them** to me..."* What is our ultimate hope in missions? Our hope is that God will do a miracle. That He will do what we cannot do. That He will draw the people we are trying to minister to towards Himself.

I will never forget the very first day Wikipai, Daapoi and I met together to begin writing lessons based on the Creation account of Genesis. They sat completely silent as if they were afraid to speak and they were going to meet their Creator for the first time face to face right then and there. They had a silent reverence and knew that something great was about to happen as I read the first verse that Jennie had translated into the Dao language. "Long long ago, in the very beginning, the Creator One created the heavens and the earth..." I read and then continued on reading... Daapoi and Wikipai looked at each other, their eyes wide as saucers. They looked back at me, their mouths slightly open as if they had just seen a ghost. They seemed almost afraid to speak. "All things? He created all the heavens and the earth? One Creator being with enough power to speak into being everything that we see? One being responsible for the sun and the moon and the stars and all that is in heavens and on the earth?" They gawked in amazement. The simplest of truths that I had heard my entire life hit them like a ton of bricks. Over and over this was their reaction as I read. - From page 256 of *Prophecies of Pale Skin*

That hope is also the very reason why this cause ultimately cannot fail and God will not be made into a liar. That is why there WILL be people "*from EVERY tongue, tribe people and nation*" standing before the throne and singing His praises at the end of time, because HE is drawing people to Himself. He has the ability to do it and is even right now drawing His elect and doing what we ourselves cannot do! He can and will do what we ourselves cannot do in this awesome task called "missions".

I had just finished reading a new section that Jennie translated for us and then "Crack! Crack!" the whole house we were sitting in began to violently jolt back and forth. I could hear some of the rafters pop and snap like they were going to split. It was another earthquake! I quickly jumped up as the floor continued to move underneath us nearly making me lose my balance. "Should we go outside? The house could fall on us!" I began to yell to Daapoi and Wikipai. They both just sat there and looked at me like I was crazy. Daapoi started to laugh and with a grin on his face said "Oh Degapiyaa, after hearing about how powerful the Creator One is all this time I am not scared of a little earthquake! I believe that God wants us to hear His message and He will not let this house fall on us because we haven't yet heard the end of His story! Sit back down and let's keep reading!" he replied... Later on that day I had flashbacks to those first foot surveys a few years back when we had seen those same men running around in circles in fear, trying to stomp on the ground to get the great "spirit snake" to leave them. What a stark contrast I had seen that morning between the way they viewed these things now and the way they had viewed them in the past. It was simple faith in the Creator. They were already beginning to taste their first bits of spiritual freedom. They were already a tiny bit at a time being set free from fears that had held their tribe captive for centuries. - From page 264 of *Prophecies of Pale Skin*

Questions

1. According to John 10:10 what does God want to give us, His creations, through Jesus and what He accomplished on our behalf? In contrast to that, what is Satan's ultimate goal for the people of this world?

2. Our world is overflowing with lesser joys that compete for our attention. There is one thing after another that our enemy would love for us to find our hope and ultimate pleasure in besides God Himself. How can we live in such a way that we model to others that Jesus is the ultimate Joy and that our ultimate hope and pleasure is in Him, not in the dry cisterns of our society?

3. In John 6:37 what does Jesus say is the reason that anyone at all comes to Him? What is one of the Father's roles in the process of salvation according to this verse?

4. In the process of salvation, what is our role and what is God's role? (1 Corinthians 3:6)

* Read **John 10:14-30** and ponder these verses and how they relate to your own life.

DAY

12

WHO
SHOULD GET
the CREDIT?

"It is not the healthy people who need a doctor, but the sick. Go and learn what this means: 'I want kindness more than I want animal sacrifices.' I did not come to invite good people but to invite sinners."

Matthew 9:12-13

Day 12: Who Should Get The Credit?

There are people we look at sometimes and think they are perhaps beyond God's grace. The murderer or rapist sitting in the prison cell, the cereal killer or terrorist insurgent that is responsible for the deaths of hundreds or even thousands of innocent people, or perhaps just the shifty eyed man that lives across the street that my wife told me makes passes at her when I am not around. We all know of people that we have such a low view of or have had so many negative experiences with that we have subconsciously written them off as beyond God's grace. In fact, maybe some of these people themselves feel as if they are beyond hope as well.

In John 7:41-43 Jesus tells an incredibly intriguing yet short and simple story about a man that had an extremely large sin debt. *"A man loaned money to two people - five hundred pieces of silver to one and fifty pieces to the other. But neither of them could repay him, so he kindly forgave them both, canceling their debts. Who do you suppose loved him more after that?" Simon answered, "I suppose the one for whom he canceled the larger debt." "That's right," Jesus said.*

> "Degapiyaa, I am old. My eyes are dark with age and my muscles have dried up. I am no longer like the other younger men. It is for this reason that I fear that when the time comes for all of us to begin hearing the Creator's message and the big talk that you have promised to tell us, I will not be able to understand these words like the others. Is it possible that this talk is one that is meant for everyone? A talk that can even be understood by the old ones? Would even an old man like me be able to hear and understand?" Obapwi asked as he fidgeted with his string bag while looking back and forth between it and then at me again. He was not the only one that had voiced these concerns to us over the past few months. Some of the women voiced their concern that this would be a talk only for the men. Some of the men even mentioned that they were concerned it would be a message too complex for the children. It seemed that the closer the time drew for everyone to gather and be taught the more nervous the people got. So many of them were so fearful that they were perhaps too backwoods or even too stupid to understand. - From page 268 of *Prophecies of Pale Skin*

This story from John 7 shows something very important about the character of Jesus. More than once, including in the first part of this chapter, Jesus was condemned by the clean cut, high and mighty religious leaders of His day for spending time with the dregs of society. In fact, He seemed to constantly surround Himself with the outcasts and immoral and spent so much time with the drinkers and the sinners that He was known by the regular synagogue goers as *"...a glutton and a drunkard, and a friend of the worst sort of sinners!"* (Luke 7:34)

It seems that Jesus viewed these types of people in a different way than we often times view them. He saw them not as people to run from, but as people to run to for the sake of the gospel. He saw His time with them as well invested and had hope for them seemingly even more so than the religious leaders of His day. He was seeking out the people that His Father draws and these were the types of social circles in which He looked for them.

"Today, you will finally hear His name" I announced as Wikipai and Daapoi sat across from me getting ready to hear the first newly translated section of scripture for the day. Their silence was nearly unbearable and the suspense had been building for weeks story after story and prophecy after prophecy from the Old testament. They had asked me time and time again in the past if I knew the name of the Redeemer Messiah that they had been waiting for... You could have heard a pin drop as I read the words to them that Jennie had finished translating just a few days before from the book of Matthew: "She gave birth to a son, and they called his name...*Yesusi*". I stopped and let them soak it in for a minute. *"Yesusi...Yesusi...Yesusi.."* they repeated over and over again to each other with a reverent whisper as if the very speaking of His name was a demonstration of such a long awaited for hope, a demonstration of the Creator's power. - From page 270 of *Prophecies of Pale Skin*

The reality is that what we see as impossible Jesus sees as possible (Mark 10:27). The people we may see as too far gone, the people with the "biggest sin debts" and those that have gotten in so much trouble and done so much bad that even if it were possible to pay for their own sins they could never in this lifetime work off all the wrong that they have done, these are the very people that according to Jesus have the possibility of "loving him more" than a person that has had a much smaller debt.

> When Wikipai and Daapoi heard about how Jesus commanded the winds and the storms to be silent and even these things obeyed His command they thought back to the stories they had heard in Genesis and Exodus about the Creator Himself. They commented that the Creator was the only other One they had heard of having power over even natural phenomena and seas. In no time at all they were saying again and again that surely Yesusi must be the Son of God because if He weren't He couldn't have done these things that only the Creator God had done in the past. When they heard His teachings and how Jesus said that he was "the trail (the way), the truth and the life" and that no one could come to the Father except by Him they were overjoyed at the thought that even Jesus Himself proclaimed that he was "the trail" to eternal life that they had been waiting for! - From page 271 of *Prophecies of Pale Skin*

The reality is that according to scripture, the sin clearing, debt-canceling salvation of our loving God is nothing short of a miracle and the forgiveness that Jesus offers is a true marvel (Matthew 19:25-26). Whether little is forgiven or much is forgiven, it takes a supernatural phenomenon for the eyes of a person to be opened to see his state and need for a Savior. The healing of a spiritually blind man is no less a miracle than the healing of physically blind man. From the wealthiest, most intelligent and advanced man in this world to the poorest, most primitive man in the jungle, the desire for salvation is a supernatural occurrence that we in and of ourselves cannot bring about. If God performs that miracle, there is salvation. If He does not, there is not (Acts 13:48).

> Daapoi as well as Wikipai were absolutely appalled at what they heard. They couldn't believe that Jesus, a man that had done nothing but good would be treated like this. They sat there with their jaws hanging open as they heard about His incredible torture by the soldiers and then His crucifixion. They were absolutely astounded at what Jesus went through. It was nearly unbearable for them to even listen to. "Degapiyaa, the words that you are telling me make my heart hurt, this is a talk that would make us cry. Jesus could have easily fled from those men or even killed them all by merely speaking a word couldn't He have? But He didn't!" Daapoi responded with anger in his voice as he heard that the nails were driven into Jesus hands and feet and then he was lifted up on the "crossed wood". As they heard up through the death of Jesus they just couldn't understand why He wouldn't fight back but instead let those people kill Him. They had seen His power demonstrated time and time again. Why wasn't He demonstrating His power just one last time and defending Himself? - From page 273 of *Prophecies of Pale Skin*

That is the reason that God Himself gets so much glory when we take Him at His word and go out to the hard places and reach out to the people that are seemingly too far gone or too backwoods to ever change.

The more dramatic the miracle the greater the fame for the Miracle Maker! And since God is the One that performs the miracle, He is the One that deserves the credit. He is the One that receives the glory. He is the One that is made famous!

> Wikipai and Daapoi heard how the Bible says that the ground shook with earthquakes and the sky was covered over with darkness at the moment that Jesus died. This was a very significant thing in Dao culture. Even when the Dao people themselves would tell a story in their language they would often talk of a natural phenomenon that had happened just before the climax of the story when the most important part was taking place... This was the Dao people's cultural way of telling the listeners that the story had hit its climax. They were cultural cues for the listeners. Likewise, when Wikipai and Daapoi heard that Jesus yelled up into the sky "Oh God, my God why have you forsaken me?" and then breathed His last breath, then the earth quaked and the veil in the temple ripped, and the skies covered over with darkness they realized what was happening. To them, this was the Creator's cue to them that His story had hit its climax, its main point! - From page 274 of *Prophecies of Pale Skin*

Too many of us get an unbiblical, man-centered savior complex when it comes to missions and evangelism. We place ourselves at the center of the picture as if we are the ones that perform the miracle that opens the eyes of the spiritually blind.

But if we are the ones that tip the scales in one direction or the other, if we as mere messengers are held up as the ones that make the ultimate difference in the hearts of our listeners, then who is it that gets the glory?

Who is it that is standing at center stage? Who is it that receives the credit for the miracle that has occurred and the change that has taken place in the listener? It is us, not God!

Daapoi was the first to respond to what he had heard. "I realize now why Yesusi didn't fight back! He took that pain for us, to become our sacrifice. If it were not for Yesusi, our wrongdoings would have never been cleared away. If Yesusi had not become the Lamb of God, sacrificed for us, we would have faced eternal punishment! I believe that this message is true, I believe that He died for me!" he replied. I could see the joy on his face as he was realizing for the first time that his past life of sin and murder had been forgiven because of what Jesus Christ had done...At this point Wikipai chimed in "If the sacrifice of Yesusi would not have been enough, God would have never raised him from the dead. If Yesusi and His sacrifice had not been enough then the curtain in the temple would have never been ripped in half to signify that we can now come into God's presence even without the sacrificial lamb. I also believe that Yesusi and His death on the crossed wood was for my wrong-doings and that His sacrifice was sufficient!"...I could see in their eyes that they had experienced the saving grace of the Great Creator and His Son Yesusi. Nothing they could do would add to it or take away from it - From pages 274-276 of *Prophecies of Pale Skin*

Beware of a view of missions and salvation that places man at the center. The one that introduces the Performer should stand to the side and the Performer of the miracle should get the praise!

After they heard about Jesus' ascension, Wikipai and Daapoi immediately began asking "When will Yesusi come back? Will He come back today? Tomorrow? Will he come back quickly?" to which I responded "Well according to the writings of Yesusi's disciples Peter and also John, He is patiently waiting for others to hear His message before He comes back. He will come back when there has been people that have believed from every language and group of people and everybody that He has called to believe has heard His message and believed." They immediately replied "Well then we have to tell the others! We have to tell our families too so that Yesusi will come back! Anybody that hasn't heard, we have to tell them His message!"...Daapoi agreed to head one direction down valley and Wikipai would head the other direction up valley. They planned on spreading the word and gathering their people! It had all come down to this. They had trusted in the finished work of Yesusi on the crossed wood and they would do everything in their power to try and bring their families, friends and relatives all throughout the Dao territory to trust in this same great Man. The Man that they had fallen in love with from the first mention of His name. This Man that had finally, through His teachings and life, given them the message that their people had so long been waiting for, the message about the one and only true "trail to eternal life". - From page 278 of *Prophecies of Pale Skin*

Questions

1. Is there anyone in your life, your family or community that you have subconsciously written off as too far gone for salvation or too far in their sin debt for anything to ever change?

2. According to Jesus, who is it that would love the Master more- the one that has been forgiven much or the one that has been forgiven little (John 7:41-43)? Why do you think Jesus made it a point to share this truth in the midst of a room holding both religious leaders and drinking sinners?

3. Why do you think the religious leaders of Jesus' day called Him *"a glutton and a drunkard, and a friend of the worst sort of sinners"* (Luke 7:34)? What did this say about their view of Jesus' ministry? Who was it that the religious leaders thought Jesus should be spending His time with if not with sinners and drunkards?

4. In light of the above questions and scriptures, if Jesus were living among us on the earth and in our community today, where do you think He would be spending a lot of His time? Who do you think He would be hanging out with? If you saw Him in these same types of places and with these types of people in modern times, do you think would you perhaps find yourself with the same attitude towards Jesus as the Pharisees had towards Him?

5. If salvation is a spiritual miracle, a supernatural occurrence which I myself as a mere message bearer cannot take credit for, who should get the glory when I lead someone to the life-giving water that is Jesus? Who should receive the praise when any individual trusts in the finished work of Jesus for their salvation?

* Read **Matthew 9:9-13** and ponder these verses and how they relate to your own life.

DAY

13

DO
you KNOW
your ROLE?

*"The ones who do the planting
or watering aren't important,
but God is important because he is
the one who makes the seed grow."*

1 Corinthians 3:7

Day 13: Do You Know Your Role?

In the Apostle Paul's day and age there was a very serious misunderstanding that unfolded in the life and body of the church. An argument which threatened to split the young fledgling Corinthian church right down the middle. These young "infant" believers as Paul calls them were absolutely ripping each other apart because of a jealousy problem. They were fighting and arguing among themselves over who their true leader should be.

"I follow Paul!" some of them said. "Well I follow Apollos!" others spoke out in disagreement. Like a couple six year olds arguing on the playground, "My dad is bigger than your dad"...."Oh yeah? My dad is stronger than your dad and he could even beat yours up if he wanted to!" to which Paul yells "Break it up you guys!" *What is Apollos? And what is Paul? We are only servants through whom you came to believe as the Lord assigned to each his task."* (1 Corinthians 3:5)

The Corinthians were missing the whole point. They were taking Paul and Apollos and placing them where they did not want to be! "Don't you dare place me on center stage! Don't even think about giving me glory for the miracle that God has done in your hearts! I don't want it!" I can hear Paul saying with heartfelt passion.

> Today would be the kick off to this much-anticipated event. Wikipai and Daapoi had done their job well! Word had spread all throughout the Dao valley and by the end of the evening it looked like everyone within a day's hike plus others from even as far as three day's hike away had gathered to hear the Creators story...To signify that this was a great event I did something that I had seen other Dao men do before as they gathered for important talks. Just as the rest of the Dao men, I had brought along my bow and arrows and my string bag also to the gathering place. Jennie and I also wore our nicest traditional nose bones for the big day, as did many of the people that had gathered to listen. Reaching over to my left I grabbed hold of my bow and arrows. I held the bow out in front of me and before saying a word, firmly held it in place with one hand while releasing the bowstring from the top of the bow with my other hand. This was a statement to the Dao people. This signified in the Dao culture that a talk was going to take place in the village that was so important that I would not even think of hunting or warfare or walking the trails on such a day. A talk so big that it was to take priority over all other events! - From page 285 of *Prophecies of Pale Skin*

The same problem that was rearing its ugly head in the Corinthian church still sneaks in and causes division in our churches today. Some men are placing others where they don't belong. Some people are giving other credit for what they in and of themselves could never do. *"Neither he who plants nor he who waters is anything, but only God, who makes things grow"* (1 Corinthians 3:7). Only God can get the ultimate credit for growth. He deserves the glory! Anything less is a lie.

As the Dao people ran out of food they would spend the weekends returning to their closest gardens to gather more so that they could continue listening to their Creators story. Some of these gardens were as far as a full day's hike away and so some mothers and fathers were carrying their children barefoot up and down four thousand foot mountains to gather food for the following week so that they could continue to listen to us teach. Many of them voiced that even though they must take these weekly trip, they felt that this was a message that was well worth it and that they would continue to make sacrifices such as these so that they could hear what the Creator had to say to them. They were making personal sacrifices and literally hiking mountains barefoot with fifty pound bags of garden foods and whatever else they could kill to eat just so that they could keep hearing the words of the Creator's leaf book. - From pages 289-290 of *Prophecies of Pale Skin*

Our role as messengers is to merely speak and to be faithful. When we try to take on the responsibility of forcing spiritual growth in another's life, we are taking on something that is not meant to be ours. We *"plant"* and we *"water"* but *"it is only God, who makes things grow"* If a single person is drawn to our message and takes it to heart then that is the supernatural power of God at work. That is His role, not ours.

When God purposes that something is going to grow, you can be assured that it will grow. As the Apostle Paul says in Philippians 1:6 *"I am confident of this, that he who began a good work in you will carry it on to completion until the day of Christ Jesus."* What God begins, He will complete! Sure, we as message bearers may have the privilege of being the mouth piece that God chooses to use to get His point across, but we cannot take glory for a person's growth any more than we can take credit for the miracle of their rebirth.

"Don't stop teaching! We want to hear more!" Every single day that we taught that first week this is what we heard...We would teach for one hour and they would want us to keep teaching for another hour. "We want you to keep teaching us until our knees are sore because we have been sitting too long!" Obapwi, one of the oldest men in the room called out from the back of the crowd after my voice had grown hoarse from talking for hours. The Dao people couldn't get enough of the Creator's message. They were excited about the things that they had heard up to that point and even though we had only been teaching for one full week it seemed that their very hearts were screaming to them that the things they were hearing were true. The majority of them expressed the same reaction that Daapoi and Wikipai had when they heard about the deception of Satan in the Garden of Eden. It was all making sense. They could look around and see evidence in their own surroundings, culture and experiences that this story was true. They could see that they also had been severely affected by the curse placed on their ancestors: the first humans, Adam and Eve. We could already see cracks forming and changes occurring in the animistic worldview of the Dao people even though theirs was a system of belief nearly thousands of years old! The words of those pages were alive! The translated portions of scripture were communicating clearly and were speaking with power! - From pages 287-288 of *Prophecies of Pale Skin*

The thing that we most often forget as messengers and missionaries is that God doesn't just use our mouths to speak His message, He uses our lives. He uses our emotions and our reactions, our joys and our sadness, our victories and our losses, our fears and our hopes, our sicknesses and our health. He uses it all to get His message across to hurting people. He uses every single bit of it for His glory.

A few days later I again contracted malaria. Those same old pounding headaches, cold sweats and constant vomiting fits were taking their toll on my body once again. The pain was incredible. "Oh God, how will I teach the people in this state?" I thought as I lay in bed in between vomiting fits...The next morning I woke up without any headaches and the nausea was gone! My fever broke in the middle of the teaching time and the listeners watched the sweat pour down my face and onto my beard and notes as I read the Old Testament portions for them that day. I had never felt this well this fast during a bout of malaria. God was watching over me and demonstrating His power to the Dao people even through our sicknesses and suffering. The Dao people were seeing the worth of our message firsthand in the fact that we continued teaching them even in the midst of physical pain and sickness. - From page 292 of *Prophecies of Pale Skin*

Even today God uses the testimonies and stories of His suffering servants to teach us about Himself. He uses Jesus' anger against the moneychangers to teach us about a passion for righteousness. He uses the joy of Jesus at the little children coming to Him to teach us about His love for humility and child like faith. He uses the sadness and weeping of Jesus at the sickness and loss of His beloved friend Lazarus to show us is His heart for those of us that He calls friends.

Some of the greatest verses in the New Testament come out of Paul's victories and losses, his fears and his hopes, his sicknesses and trials. *"To live is Christ and to die is gain!"* Paul spoke out in reply to his circumstances in a dark, cold prison cell, while his hands and feet were chained because of his faithful proclamation of the gospel (Philippians 1:21). Be assured that God is not only using our words to speak His message, He is using our lives.

We don't only speak great things about God, we live them! Since the beginning of time itself, God has been sovereignly working together His unwavering plan to see representatives from every last tongue, nation, tribe and people standing before His throne on that final day. And not only do our mouths have a role to play in the proclamation of the cross and the advancement of the kingdom but even more importantly, so do our lives and our sufferings.

"It is finished!" they heard Yesusi yell out as He breathed His last breath and then hung there on that crossed wood limp and lifeless. The earth shook with earthquakes and the darkness moved in. The sky rumbled and the veil in the temple ripped. Then finally, all in a moment the lights began to come on for many of the listeners. Just as Wikipai and Daapoi had in the months before, so many of the other Dao listeners recognized the earthquakes, darkness and other unusual natural phenomena during the death of Christ as signs from their Creator that the climax of the story had been reached! We continued on explaining through the burial of Yesusi in a rich man's tomb and how not a single one of His bones had been broken during His gruesome crucifixion. They recognized one Old Testament prophecy after another that He had fulfilled and started smiling and talking among themselves as they listened. As I continued to teach and read from the final lesson I began hearing the hum of excited chatter in the room as the Dao people began making comments to one another about what they were hearing.
- From page 305 of *Prophecies of Pale Skin*

Jesus' sufferings were the exclamation point of His love for us. They were the climax of God's story of salvation. Our sufferings are our exclamation point to those we minister to of the authenticity of our message. They are the climax of our testimony to them.

Only eight verses after Paul uttered those iconic words *"for me to live is Christ, and to die is gain"* and while the cold steel chains still hung from his wrists, he continued on *"Don't be frightened....For it has been granted to you on behalf of Christ not only to believe on him, but also to suffer for him"* (Philippians 1:28-29). Salvation is not the only gift that God grants. There is something else that God also sovereignly grants to us for the sake of His glory and the ultimate good of His people-it is suffering.

> When I told them of how the followers of Yesusi discovered the stone from the tomb rolled to the side and also discovered Him risen from the dead some of the Dao listeners seemed as if they could hardly contain themselves any longer! "What do you have to say about what you are hearing? Go ahead, speak it out!" I encouraged them. "It's true! This is a true talk! Yesusi has cleared away our wrong doings!" shouted Totopwi. Then Wusimpaa, Apiyaawogi, and Obapwi started to chime in: "I believe this is true as well! I also believe! Yesusi is the Son of God!" Another man spoke out...People continued to excitedly add in from all over the crowd. They broke out into a spontaneous time of testimony, some of them standing up to share their personal belief in what Christ had done with the rest of the group, while others just listened and grinned from ear to ear while nodding in agreement. They were right in front of our eyes expressing faith in the sacrifice of Yesusi on the crossed wood. They were speaking out about what Jesus has done on their behalf... We couldn't help but smile as we watched God doing what Jesus said in Mark chapter ten was "humanly impossible" for we ourselves to do. We didn't stop at the end of the final lesson and asked anybody to "Pray a special sinners prayer" or "Repeat these special words after me". We didn't tell them that there were any special weekly rituals they needed to perform for God's approval or that from now on they would have to dress like foreigners and stop smoking their tobacco or drinking certain drinks. There was no talk of leaving behind their traditional dress and nose bones or their bows and arrows. They knew as well as we did that the sacrifice of Jesus was completely sufficient. It was all about what He had accomplished for them on that crossed wood and no one could take this away from them! It was a miracle that God had done in the hearts of the Dao people right before our very eyes. It was a miracle that only the great Creator Himself could have done! - From pages 306-307 of *Prophecies of Pale Skin*

Ever since the cross, time and time again God has used the sufferings of His messengers to usher in salvation to the lost. To embrace the hardship and suffering that God has granted to us in the same way that Jesus did is to place God and His glory at center stage. To embrace the suffering that God has given us to embrace is to say to a dying world *"Neither he who plants nor he who waters is anything!"* It is to live saying, "I am nothing! God is everything!"

Questions

1. Who should get the glory when any single person turns and places their trust in the sacrifice of Christ after we have shared with them the gospel? According to Paul, why should God get the glory? (1 Corinthians 3:5-7)

2. What is the result when we take on a role that is not ours and in turn try to force growth in our listeners? If we try to take that responsibility on our shoulders, and if no growth occurs in our listener's hearts how does that make us feel about ourselves?

3. In Philippians 1:6 Paul tells us that if God begins a good work in an individual, He will be faithful to complete it. How is this truth freeing for us as mere messengers? How should this truth affect our view of God's involvement in the growth of our listeners?

4. What does God use to get His message and point across to our listeners just as much as our mouths? Why is it important that my life matches my message?

5. Paul tells us that the ability to believe the gospel is not the only thing that God has granted to us. There is something else that He also grants to us for His own glory. What is it? (Philippians 1:28-29)

* Read **Matthew 9:9-13** and ponder these verses and how they relate to your own life.

DAY

14

WHAT
is SO
IMPORTANT?

"Those things were important to me, but now I think they are worth nothing because of Christ... I think that all things are worth nothing compared with the greatness of knowing Christ Jesus my Lord. Because of him, I have lost all those things, and now I know they are worthless trash."

Philippians 3:7-8

Day 14: What Is So Important?

In the same way that a match is struck in the cold darkness and held high above ones head so that the things in the shadows can be exposed for what they really are, when God Himself becomes everything to us and we hold Him up as our greatest Treasure, the lesser joys in the cold, dark corners of our lives are unveiled in the midst of the darkness and we begin to finally see them as the insignificant little trinkets that they really are.

"I thought I would never live long enough to hear this talk. I thought that I was too old already and that I would die before you had ever learned our language well enough to speak to us this great message that I have heard over these past couple moons. I used to think 'Well, I will not get to hear the big talk, but at least my children and grandchildren will get to hear it and will know the trail to God's good place above the sky.' But now I have heard the Creator's message to us. I have heard of His Son Yesusi and what He has done for me and it is good! Jesus paid for our wrong doings on that crossed wood and I believe He did that for me."...Now, the prophetic dreams given to his people long before we ever arrived had come true, we were brothers! Totopwi had become part of God's family - From page 310 of *Prophecies of Pale Skin*

When we truly embrace God's word as our ultimate authority, it revolutionizes our lives. We suddenly have a firm foundation to stand on when all we ever knew up to that point was the unstable mud and mire through which we were trudging day after day. Things begin to make sense that never made sense to us before and things that once seemed important to us just don't seem as important anymore.

The Apostle Paul describes the same thing as happening to him when Jesus saved him from the religious culture of his own day; *"I am a Hebrew, and my parents were Hebrews. I had a strict view of the law, which is why I became a Pharisee. I was so enthusiastic I tried to hurt the church. No one could find fault with the way I obeyed the law of Moses.* **Those things were important to me**, *but now I think they are worth nothing because of Christ.* **Not only those things, but I think that all things are worth nothing compared with the**

greatness of knowing Christ Jesus my Lord, *Because of him, I have lost all those things, and now I know they are worthless trash. This allows me to have Christ"* (Philippians 3:5-8). The secondary affections Paul had pursued so hard in the past became to him as a big pile of stinking garbage. They didn't even compare to his one ultimate possession and passion- Jesus Christ. The person and work of Jesus had become everything to Paul and God's word had become Paul's guide for everything he did and every decision he made.

As we continued on through the book of Acts the new believers saw that the early church had baptized people as a sign to the community that they were following Jesus now. The Dao people likewise wanted to follow this example. They had come to the conclusion that whatever the early church in the Creator's leaf book had done was what they also wanted to do... They had made clear to us in the past that they believed there was a specific powerful female evil spirit that lived in the rivers and would do them harm should they bathe or spend time near certain streams. This was one of the main reasons why they seldom bathed or washed their cuts and were usually caked with dirt and ash from the fires. This was an age-old belief and fear that had a grip on the Dao people for literally thousands of years before we ever arrived... However, to our surprise and despite the age old fears they had of a female evil spirit living in the waters, the Dao believers stepped forward one at a time to be baptized in testimony of their faith in the sacrifice of Yesusi... The Dao people also saw in the book of Acts that the first group of believers had also regularly taken communion together in remembrance and honor of Jesus and what He had accomplished. They wanted to share the "wine" and "bread" together in remembrance of what Jesus has done for them just like the early church. In these jungles however, it was nearly impossible to come up with things such as wine and bread. After thinking and talking about it, some of the men got together and decided that sweet potatoes and water would have to suffice seeing as how it is the remembrance of what Yesusi has done that is the key issue, not the actual wine and bread. - From page 313-314 of *Prophecies of Pale Skin*

Any fear of death Paul once may have had completely lost its power and he called death *"Gain"* (Philippians) because the very consummation of his joy awaited him on the other side of death, in his Savior's embrace. His ultimate joy had once been in the approval of the Pharisee and men on his right and left, his pride had been in his pure Jewish roots and his strict adherence to the religious culture and system. *"I am a Hebrew, and my parents were*

Hebrews. I had a strict view of the law, which is why I became a Pharisee. I was so enthusiastic I tried to hurt the church. No one could find fault with the way I obeyed the law of Moses. Those things were important to me..." (Philippians 3:5-6). Now his ultimate joy was in only one Man. His Jewish roots, the approval of high and mighty religious leaders, and the religious culture he grew up in meant nothing to him. *"Those things were important to me, but now I think they are worth nothing because of Christ."*

> Things were dramatically changing in the Dao valley. The people were struggling to sift through their old ways and expose those practices that went against the Creator's book and at the same time continue on with those cultural practices that didn't. Old beliefs were being weekly challenged as they learned more and more and heard the stories of the early church in the New Testament. Some of the believers were stepping forward and boldly calling out those old rituals that didn't line up with the things they were hearing in the Creators book... "Creator One, You are greater than the greatest, You are bigger than the biggest! You are more powerful than the most powerful! And we know that there is nothing that You cannot do! Today we that have gathered here are afraid of the evil spirits and because we know that Yesusi has the power to cause these evil spirits to flee from this place, we are asking You to protect us and cause them to leave! Thank you Yesusi for watching over us. Please continue to watch over us because only You are the One that can do anything." Wikipai prayed out in the middle of all those gathered. - From pages 318-322 of *Prophecies of Pale Skin*

Jesus Christ was giving Paul a true, pure refreshing satisfaction that the hollow, dry, sand-filled cistern of religion and pride and man's approval could never give him. And once he had tasted that sweet spring in the desert that is only God Himself, there could be no turning back. The old system had been exposed for what it really was and Jesus had also truly been shown for the ultimate Treasure that He truly is.

Paul had a new goal in his sights and he reveals it only three verses later; *"I want to know Christ and the power that raised him from the dead. I want to share in his sufferings and become like him in his death" Philippians 3:10.* He was willing to give anything, to experience anything if it only meant he could experience Jesus Christ just a little bit more. He was hooked! He just couldn't get enough of that crystal clear sweet Water. If it were possible to buy it he would have given his last penny for just one more sip. He was so crazy about and addicted to Jesus that he nearly couldn't talk about anything else.

> Another thing that there was a huge push for along that time in the Dao people group was for literacy programs to be taught and for anyone that was able, to learn how to read and write. We had talked to some of them about the importance of reading but it didn't seem that they really saw the need for learning how to read until they had begun to hear and understand the stories from the Creator's book. They began to see that if they put the time into learning this new ability, to understand the markings on a page, they would soon be able to read the Creator's leaf book for themselves whenever they wanted to! At the point that they understood that one simple truth, the literacy program began to absolutely take off!.. Now everybody in the village, both old and young, literate and illiterate had a way to hear stories from the Creator's leaf book in their own gardens and houses! These little books and scripture portions that Jennie had worked so hard to translate and I had labored to teach were now being regularly carried in the string bags of the Dao people for miles upon miles and read all over the Dao territory. Daapoi summed it up well when at one of the weekly gatherings he stated to all those gathered: "Just as our garden food provides nourishment for the stomach and makes us strong, the Creator's leaf book and His words within it are like the sweet potato for our souls by which our souls can become strong and we can live well."
> - From page 317 of *Prophecies of Pale Skin*

So where did this new passion for Jesus alone take Paul? What did Paul reap from his pursuit of this one Man, this ultimate Treasure? When it was all said and done, what had he traded this "garbage" that he once held so dear in for?

If we look at this question from a mere physical perspective we can confidently say that he traded it in for hardship after hardship. *"I have worked much harder, been in prison more frequently, been flogged more severely, and been exposed to death again and again. Five times I received from the Jews the forty lashes minus one. Three times I was beaten with rods, once I was stoned, three times I was shipwrecked, I spent a night and a day in the open sea, I have been constantly on the move. I have been in danger from rivers, in danger from bandits, in danger from my own countrymen, in danger from Gentiles; in danger in the city, in danger in the country, in danger at sea; and in danger from false brothers. I have labored and toiled and have often gone without sleep; I have known hunger and thirst and have often gone without food; I have been cold and naked" (2 Corinthians 11:23-27).* Paul's wish to share in the sufferings of Christ had no doubt become a reality.

But if we look at what Paul gained from a spiritual perspective we can confidently say that he traded that "garbage" for joy upon joy! *"...I am full of joy over you"* (Romans 16:19), *"In all our troubles my joy knows no bounds!"* (2 Corinthians 7:4), *"My joy was greater than ever..."* (2 Corinthians 7:7), *"I always pray with joy..."* (Philippians 1:4), *"How can we thank God enough for you in return for all the joy we have in the presence of our God because of you?"* (1 Thessalonians 3:9), *"Your love has given me great joy and encouragement"* (Philemon 1:7).

Because his greatest pleasure was in Jesus himself and his goal was to know Jesus and to travel to places *"where Christ had never been named and no church has been established"* (Romans 15:20) to make Jesus known, Paul was able to say that even despite all of his troubles, the fact that he was seeing people changed by the gospel and Jesus Christ being made known made his joy know no bounds. Over and over and over again he had the joy of witnessing firsthand people kneeling at the refreshing Spring that is Jesus and taking their first drink and being changed forever because of it.

> God was doing great things in the Dao valley and proving His power over and over again to the Dao people. Jennie and I had never seen anything like it before even back in America. Even our faith was being strengthened because of what we saw God doing for the Dao people! - From page 324 of *Prophecies of Pale Skin*
>
> One of the first big events that the Dao people wanted to celebrate after they heard the Creator's talk that first time was Christmas... They called it in their language the *"Yesusi onee daata naagoo"* which translated means "The day that Jesus' cord was cut."... "If the day the cord of Yesusi was cut had never taken place, how different things would be for us Dao people today! We would even now be living as if we didn't have any eyes. In fact we would be as a person without any head at all because we would be as those who couldn't see, couldn't hear about, believe, or even follow the good trail that Yesusi brought us, the trail that leads to eternal life!" we heard one young believer speak out to all the others during the first Christmas celebration to ever occur in the Dao Tribe. - From pages 329-330 of *Prophecies of Pale Skin*

Jesus turned Paul's life upside down. He used to travel the known world trying to imprison and murder others, now he was traveling the world trying to set people free and usher in to them the only Source of spiritual life! And Jesus has been doing this same amazing thing with people ever since. He is taking murderers, thieves, drunkards and sinners, healing their spiritually blind eyes, clearing their sin debts and sending them back out again to revolutionize their cities and communities for the glory of His Father and the eternal joy of His people!

> (After the war party came through our village)...Uwokaatoma, in representation of all of the believers that had gathered to hear God's word that Sunday prayed for their enemies and pleaded with His Creator. "Oh Creator One, please see our situation, change our enemies hearts, please take away their hatred and their desire to kill us. Please take away their wanting to shoot us with their arrows. We know now that they only do these things because they have not yet heard Your message and that in the past we were no different than them. *Forgive them because they don't know what they are doing.* Take the hate from their hearts as You have taken the hate from our hearts. Change them as You have changed us."... His prayer was so different from anything Jennie or I had ever seen or heard growing up in the church back in America. Even at the very moment Uwokaatoma was crying these words out our "Christian" country was sending more troops to Middle Eastern countries in retaliation for their attacks on us....With tears in our eyes, Jennie and I walked back to our little jungle house that day realizing that our attitude and the attitude of most of those from our own country had not been the attitude of Jesus. As we walked down the jungle trail, we asked God to change us and thanked Him that even though some might all us "missionaries" to the Dao people, God was actually now using the Dao people to reach and change us. - From page 327 of *Prophecies of Pale Skin*

Once the match has been struck in the cold darkness and has been held high above one's head so that the entire community in a dark place can see for the first time, how worthless the little trinkets they have been chasing after really are, that community will never be the same. The worthless things in the shadows have been exposed and they pale in comparison to the greatest Treasure of all that is Jesus.

As Totopwi looked around at his sons and family and at the others sitting around the room. In a weak voice he began: "The Creator's talk is big and there is nothing bigger. I will soon die and my spirit will not carry with it any of my belongings. I will leave all of my shell money behind. I will leave my pigs and my gardens and my houses and my wives also behind. Nothing will go with me, not even my body. My spirit will go up alone. All of those things I once thought so important will no longer even belong to me and so I say to you hold onto the words of the Creator's leaf book and never let them go! Do not run after those other things that you also will leave behind when you die someday. Instead run after and hold onto the Creator's talk because your spirit is the only thing that will go up to heaven in the end."...During the following night Totopwi's spirit left his body and went up to be with his Creator just as he had foretold. The dream he had experienced the evening before had been prophetic just as he told us and the others the day before his death. Both believers and unbelievers all over the Dao territory heard the story of Totopwi's prophetic dream and his last words. People from miles around hiked to his village and gathered to mourn his death and it was an incredible time of testimony for the entire tribe. The dream that Totopwi had so boldly talked about, in which Jesus was personified as the only ladder to the Creators good place above the sky was a clear message to him, his family and the entire tribe that there is only one ladder, one trail, and one way to eternal life: the Great Creator's only Son Yesusi. - From page 332 of *Prophecies of Pale Skin*

Questions

1. Is there a difference in your life in between what you used to hold up as so important before you trusted in the work of Jesus Christ and what you hold up as important now? (Philippians 3:7)

2. Have the things you used to live for become as "*garbage*" to you as in comparison to your desire to "*know Christ*" as they did for Paul? If not, why not? (Philippians 3:8)

3. Has Jesus become to you like a cool, sweet spring that you just can't get enough of or something that you have to force yourself to drink just a little bit more of?

4. Are you holding Jesus up in your community as your greatest Treasure? Or have other, less important things taken His place in your life? What is it that is the most important to you?

* Read **Ephesians 5:8** and ponder this verse and how it relates to your own life.

DAY

15

WHICH MASTER RULES YOU?

*"Wherever your treasure is,
there your heart and thoughts
will also be."*

-Matthew 6:21

Day 15: Which Master Rules You?

"No man can serve two masters" Jesus told His disciples. He had just finished explaining to them what will happen to their treasures if they choose to *"store them up on earth, where moth and rust destroy, and where thieves break in and steal"* (Matthew 6:19-20). "You will lose it all!" Jesus says and then He goes on to answer a very important question.

 What is the result if a man doesn't take Jesus' advice? What if a person tries to serve two masters anyway? What will be the result? Can it really hurt anything if I make God's glory my aim most of the time but make my own comfort my priority the rest? If I try to serve both masters instead of devoting everything solely to one, what will eventually happen? *"Either you will hate one master and love the other or you will be devoted to the one and despise the other"* Jesus replies. (Matthew 6:24)

"No man can serve two masters" Jesus says. Don't even try because in the end it will ruin you. You will be standing at the conclusion of your life, only moments before you meet your Creator face to face, with nothing but handfuls of corroded, moth eaten and tarnished trinkets that you will have to leave behind. And when it finally strikes you that all you have invested your life in is worthless, with tears in your eyes you will say "If only I could do it all over again...If only I had another chance...If only.....If only......"

"No man can serve two masters". If you give everything you have to serve the true Master, the one and only true King, just like the Apostle Paul and so many others, you may find that life is filled with hardship and trials. But just like Paul and so many others you will also find that these very trials and sufferings are nothing more than mere servants which bring you what you desire the most. The pains of this world will be nothing more than a path to experiencing the ultimate Pleasure - God Himself.

It was still the same beautiful, intriguing, yet hard to get along with remote jungle. The same incredibly steep mountains and muddy trails. The same leeches, mosquitos, malaria and jungle sicknesses, but everything had changed. The people used to sit on our porches for hours talking about only string bags, pigs and shell money. Now there was a core group of people for whom a new thing seemed to dominate the majority of their conversation. Sure, they still sometimes talked about all the same things of the Dao culture that others were talking about, but all these other everyday things were merely second priority to the greatest thing. They knew the reason all these other things existed. They knew that all these things were because of their Creator and they knew that none of these things held a candle in comparison to their greatest Treasure, Yesusi!...We finally had true, deep fellowship with many of the Dao people that we had never had before. The prophecies of their ancestors had really come true: "Though our skin was pale and we came from a far away land, after they heard our message, we had become like brothers and sisters with one another. We were like family."- From page 336 of *Prophecies of Pale Skin*

God is working out His plan to see the last of the last brought into the sheepfold. *"I am the good shepherd; I know my sheep and my sheep know me, just as the Father knows me and I know the Father and I lay down my life for the sheep. I have other sheep that are not of this sheep pen. I **must** bring them also. They too will listen to my voice, and there shall be one flock and one shepherd"* (John 10:14-16).

Jesus does not say "I might bring them" He says "*I must bring them*"! Every last sheep which the Father has appointed and given to Jesus MUST and WILL be brought in. His plan WILL be accomplished and He has given us the incredible privilege of being a part of His plan to gather every last sheep that are scattered all over the face of the earth. We have the "joy" as Paul called it of seeing firsthand people brought into the fold and changed by the gospel of Jesus.

Wikipai gathered a handful of dirty, crooked twigs from the ground and placed them inside a clean straight hollow piece of bamboo. "This is what Yesusi accomplished for us when we trusted in what He has done for us on the crossed wood. Though we were dirty, crooked and sinful in the Creator's sight, because we are in Yesusi we now are seen by our Creator as straight and new. We are clean in the Creator's sight because of what Yesusi has done." Wikipai concluded. The listeners always laughed with joy when we shared illustrations like this. God was speaking through the things of their surroundings and culture and they loved it! Many of them were growing in their understanding of Jesus. - From page 337 of *Prophecies of Pale Skin*

We have the awesome experience of seeing people being ripped free from the hands of their old master who desired nothing but harm, death and destruction for them and embraced in the arms of their loving Creator who desires nothing for them but *"life and life more abundantly"* (John 10:10).

Does this mean that we can expect nothing but health, wealth and prosperity for those that we point towards the fold and whom in turn Jesus brings into it? After looking at the example of what happened to Paul, what church history says happened to nearly every other one of Jesus' disciples and most importantly to the example of Jesus Christ Himself in His suffering, we would be foolish to come to that conclusion. The Bible is clear that *"all those who desire to live godly lives in Christ Jesus will suffer persecution"* (2 Timothy 3:12).

> "How can you sit there and speak so confidently about what will happen to our spirits! I am sick of hearing about it!" shouted Magabeotoma. "These are not my words older brother, they are the Creator's words. That is how I know these things will happen! And I will never stop talking about the Creator and His message here or anywhere else!" replied Daapoi. Magabeotoma had hit his bursting point, he couldn't believe what he was hearing!... He dropped the club and went for his bow and arrows. Within seconds he had an arrow pulled back in his bow, pointed directly at Daapoi and angrily yelled "I will not just strike you younger brother! I will kill you! Do not ever speak of these things here again!" With his older brother Magabeotoma's bow drawn and the sharp bamboo tipped arrow pointed directly at his chest from only a few feet away Daapoi gave one final reply: "I cannot and will not stop preaching the Creator's words. I do not fear death and what you are doing right now to me is no different from what happened in between Abel and his older brother Cain. You are my older brother and you like Cain have chosen not to follow the Creator. I am like Abel and I have chosen to follow and believe the Creator's words and so you want to kill me. So go ahead and shoot! In the future, when you and I are both dead and gone and standing before the Creator, you will see that His words are true!" - From pages 339-340 of *Prophecies of Pale Skin*

Again, these words don't say we "might suffer persecution" they say we "*WILL suffer persecution*". Suffering is not an option. It is not something to run from. It is something to expect not only for ourselves but for our spiritual children as well. The suffering servants of today that are persecuted for the advancement of the gospel and the martyrs of our generation that lay down their lives for the glory of our King are the ones that step into eternity with joy and confidence as they meet their Creator face to face. They walk across the finish line not to the sound of the corroded, moth eaten, tarnished trinkets that they cherished falling from their hands and hitting the ground but to the sound of their Master's welcoming voice saying "*well done my good and faithful servant*" and into the embrace of the only Treasure that really ever truly made them happy to begin with. (Matthew 25:21)

I will never forget seeing Wikipai smiling up at me from the little lean to beside that jungle stream. The image is burned in my mind like a still photograph. We hadn't realized how serious things were until we finally made it down to Taomi and caught our first glimpse of his sickness worn, emaciated body. To this day there isn't nearly a week that goes by that I still don't think about those words that he said to us. With the little bit of strength he had remaining in his body he had said those words to us in almost a whisper. *"Oh friend, do not cry for me. Do not cry for me. Yes, it is true that my body is wasting away. I am like a jungle stream that has not been fed by the rain for many days, but although my body is very weak, my spirit is strong. I know what the Creator One's Son has done for me. And if I die here in this place then the Creator One has chosen that for me. I am ready to go... do not cry for me."* He said every word with such a sweet smile on his face. - From pages 344-345 of *Prophecies of Pale Skin*

It is hard to say goodbye. It is hard to watch the ones we have grown to love walk away and into the long, beautiful hall of eternity. This curse of sin and death that has been placed on humanity in not an easy one to bear. But thanks to our King, *"death has been swallowed up in victory...because He gives us victory through our Lord Jesus Christ"!* (1 Corinthians 15:54-58)

We no longer grieve like *"those who grieve as if they have no hope"* because we know without a doubt that "*the Lord himself will come down from heaven with a loud command, with the voice of the archangel, and with the trumpet call of God. And those who have died believing in Christ will rise first. After that, we who are still alive will be gathered up with them in the clouds to meet the Lord in the air. And we will be with the Lord forever"* (1 Thessalonians 4:13-18).

"God You have to heal him!" I pleaded over and over again under my breath for hours as we made our way farther and farther up into the mountains. Finally we made it back up to Wikipai's village..."Surely God wouldn't take Wikipai of all people!" I reasoned with myself but even after we made it back up to the highlands and were able to get him back to his village, he wasn't recovering. Day after day I spent nearly all day sitting with him, cooking for him and trying to administer medicine. *"No man knows the day that I will die, but the Creator knows. Will I die soon while I still am young? Will I die while my wife and I have only cut the cords of two children? Will I die when I am old and have lived a good long life? No man can know such things, but the Creator knows. And if I die while I am still young, then the Creator has chosen that for me. I am ready to go up to that good place above the sky and live with Yesusi."* Wikipai said to me as I sat with him next to the fire in his little thatch roofed house. Then a little while later he lay down on his weaved leaf mat and breathed his last breath. - From page 346 of *Prophecies of Pale Skin*

Time and time again we have to be reminded that we don't know what is best and that our place isn't to try to be the managers of God's glory. God knows what He is doing and He is working out every detail for the joy of His people and the sake of His reputation. He will not be made into a liar. His plan, which was laid out clearly for us in Isaiah 52:15 nearly three thousand years ago will not fail. Our place is to simply be a part of that plan. Our responsibility is to go where our Master tells us to go and to speak when He tells us to speak. He will be faithful to do the rest.

In that moment I realized that if there was any one thing I had learned during those past few months as I had watched Wikipai spend his last days trying to carry God's message to the people that had not yet had a chance to hear, then in the midst of his efforts slowly waste away in his sickness but never stop smiling and giving God glory despite his suffering, I had learned what it looks like to die well. Because when I die, I want my last weeks to have been spent on the front lines. I want my last days to have been spent commending Jesus to the most unreached of the unreached with a smile on my face no matter how much pain I may be in. And I want my last words to have been spent pointing my family, friends, brothers, sisters and all those around me towards our Creator so that He is the One people are left looking at, not me. Then a smile stretched across my face as I thought about how great it will be to someday be reunited with Wikipai and Totopwi again. - From pages 350 of *Prophecies of Pale Skin*

How awesome that day will be when this battle is finally over and Jesus has decided that the job is done! Jennie and I will be standing side by side with many Dao people, many of our family and a vast sea of people from every language group, tribe, people and nation as the book of Revelation describes and we will all be together singing out heartfelt praises with everything inside of us to Yesusi for what He has done for us on that crossed wood. It isn't until then that the best will have arrived because it is then that we will experience more joy and satisfaction in our beings than we have ever experienced before. It is on that awesome day that our great Creator will finally get the glory He deserves. These present trials will be well worth the enjoyment that is yet to come. We haven't barely even begun to experience true life yet! - From page 350 of *Prophecies of Pale Skin*

Questions

1. Which master do you serve? If you say that King Jesus is your Master, does your heart, thoughts and lifestyle agree with what you are saying? What and who do your heart and thoughts say that your true treasure and true master is?

2. What does Jesus tell us will happen to us if we try to spend this life serving two masters? (Matthew 6:24)

3. What does Jesus say about the sheep that have not yet been brought into the fold? Does He say he "might" bring them in or that He "*must*" bring them in? What does this victorious truth mean for those of us that are seeking to be a part of God's agenda and are going out to see God's elect gathered from every tongue, tribe, people and nation? (John 10:14-16)

4. What does 2 Timothy 3:12 say we can expect in relation to suffering persecution? Does this verse say that those of us who desire to live godly lives "might" suffer persecution or that all those who desire to live godly lives "*will*" suffer persecution? What does this mean for us that are taking God at His word, trying to live godly lives, and going out to the hard places for the sake of the advancement of the gospel?

5. According to 1 Corinthians 15:54-58 and also 1 Thessalonians 4:13-18, why is it that even in the hard circumstances when we see friends, family and our spiritual children suffering and perhaps even dying for the sake of the gospel, we can still have hope? Who is it that gives us the ultimate victory regardless of the circumstances?

* Read **Luke 18:18-30** and ponder these verses and how they relate to your own life.

CONCLUDING WORDS

"Wow....I had no idea! I did not know that those are the type of challenges front lines foreign missionaries face to carry the message of Jesus to new places. In fact, I didn't even know areas that remote and untouched with truth still exist!" This is the type of reaction I have gotten over and over again from individuals and even some of my close friends and family that have read the book *Prophecies of Pale Skin*.

As more and more people have read our story and some have started writing reviews online and elsewhere, many different individuals have penned the following types of statements: *"Prophecies of Pale Skin has helped me to better understand how to pray for our front lines overseas missionaries serving in third world, remote areas and primarily unreached Muslim countries. The things written about in the book gave me a new insider's perspective into the trials, challenges and needs that our modern day missionaries face. They also serve as a reminder that God is alive and active today and doing awesome things to see His message carried to the last remaining unreached people groups scattered around the world."*

The book *Prophecies of Pale Skin* is the incredible account of the things God has done in the remote Dao tribe of Indonesia, and this book, *The Leaf Book and the Crossed Wood* is about the unique and amazing things that God has been teaching both the Dao people and our family through what He has been doing. It is my hope that through these books you have been dramatically challenged in your own faith and perspective.

My heartfelt desire is that you have been challenged not only in your perspective regarding the missionaries that you or your church may be praying for and supporting, but also that your perspective has been challenged in regards to yourself and the part that you can play in seeing God's fame spread throughout the nations. God has a plan for you in His grand scheme of bringing in *"representatives from every tongue, tribe, people and nation"* (Revelation 5:9).

It is my sincere prayer that as you have followed this study you have gained a fresh perspective and that a new passion has been kindled in your heart to be a part of the awesome things that God is doing in this world. It is my hope that you have grasped a new understanding of how you can not only pray for and stand behind our foreign missionaries that have been duking it out on the front lines but also how you can come alongside of them and encourage them and perhaps even play a greater part in getting the gospel to the last remaining deepest and darkest corners of this world for the glory of our great God!

Right now, as you read the words on this page, there are those that are laying everything on the line for our message. There are those that have been through so much that they feel ready to give up and call it quits. There are foreign missionaries in many different places that feel as though they are barely hanging on by a thread. They need encouragement and new strength to re-grip the torch that they feel is about to slip from their hands. As they struggle forward they need new empowering from the only One that can ultimately sustain and strengthen them in this awesome task. They need God to do a miracle in their hearts that only He can do, a miracle that can be ushered in by the prayers of His people. (2 Thessalonians 1:11) God has a role for you to fill in this awesome task. You are not exempt from His call to "*go into all the world...*" anymore than the disciples themselves were. Only three options lay before you: you can go yourself, send others and stand behind them through your prayers and support, or you can be disobedient to our King. Which part will you play?

If you have a desire to play a part specifically through supporting our family in our ongoing efforts here in Indonesia and in the Dao tribe, you can contact us or get involved with our work through our website:

propheciesofpaleskin.org

SCRIPTURE INDEX

Chapter 1: What Is Your Greatest Joy?

1. John 4:14

2. Luke 12:16-21

3. Luke 12:33-34

Chapter 2: What Is Your Source Of Hope?

1. Titus 3:5-6

2. 2 Timothy 3:5

3. Matthew 23:15

4. Numbers 22:21-41

5. 1 Corinthians 15:1-5

6. John 6:44

Chapter 3: What Is God's Agenda?

1. Matthew 28:18-20

2. Romans 15:20-22

3. Isaiah 52:15

Chapter 4: Is It Worth It?

1. 1 Peter 4:13

2. Mark 14:36

3. Hebrews 12:1-4

Chapter 5: What Will It Cost?

1. Galatians 3:26-28

2. Luke 9:58

3. John 17

4. John 20

5. 1 Peter 3:15

6. Matthew 16:24-26

Chapter 6: Does God Know What He Is Doing?

1. 1 Corinthians 1:27-31

2. 1 Samuel 17

3. Exodus 4:10-15

4. Acts 4:13

5. Acts 17:6

6. 2 Corinthians 12:7

7. 2 Corinthians 12:9

8. Matthew 13:55

Chapter 7: What If It Was You?

1. Psalm 36:9

2. Jonah 4:11

3. John 3:16

4. 2 Corinthians 4:3-6

Chapter 8: Is God A Liar?

1. Revelation 7:9-10

2. Hebrews 6:18

3. Isaiah 48:9-11

4. James 2:19

5. Isaiah 55:11

6. Psalm 67

Chapter 9: Culture Or Christ, Which One Is King?

1. 1 Corinthians 9:20-23

2. Hebrews 2:14-18

3. John 20:27

4. John 15:13

5. Isaiah 53

6. 1 Peter 4:1

7. 1 Corinthians 9:20-23

8. Matthew 15:1-20

Chapter 10: Have We Settled For A Substitute?

1. Romans 1:21-32

2. Jeremiah 2:13

3. Matthew 13:44-48

Chapter 11: What Is It That We Cannot Do?

1. John 10:10

2. John 4:10

3. John 6:37

4. John 6:44

5. John 10:14-30

Chapter 12: Who Should Get The Credit?

1. Matthew 9:12-13

2. John 7:41-43

3. Luke 7:34

4. Mark 10:27

5. Matthew 19:25-26

6. Acts 13:48

7. Matthew 9:9-13

Chapter 13: Do You Know Your Role?

1. 1 Corinthians 3:7

2. 1 Corinthians 3:5

3. Philippians 1:21

4. Philippians 1:6

5. Philippians 1:28-29

6. Matthew 9:9-13

Chapter 14: What Is So Important To You?

1. Philippians 3:5-8

2. Philippians 3:10

3. 2 Corinthians 11:23-27

4. Romans 16:19

5. 2 Corinthians 7:4

6. 2 Corinthians 7:7

7. Philippians 1:4

8. 1 Thessalonians 3:9

9. Philemon 1:7

10. Romans 15:20

11. Ephesians 5:8

Chapter 15: Which Master Rules You?

1. Matthew 6:21

2. Matthew 6:19-20

3. Matthew 6:24

4. John 10:14-16

5. John 10:10

6. 2 Timothy 3:12

7. Matthew 25:21

8. 1 Corinthians 15:54-58

9. 1 Thessalonians 4:13-18

10. Isaiah 52:15

11. Luke 18:18-30

Concluding Words

1. Revelation 5:9

2. 2 Thessalonians 1:1

ABOUT THE AUTHOR

D.S. PHILLIPS is a translator, literacy teacher and church planter who holds multiple degrees in both Intercultural and Biblical Studies. He and his family have been living in Indonesia for over a decade, laboring to see unreached people groups have their first opportunity to hear about their Creator and what He has done for them.

They have spent most of their time living and working among the very remote Dao tribe, a people group that before they arrived had no written alphabet for their dialect, not a single verse of scripture available to them and no church or religious organization of any type working among them.

D.S. Phillips and his wife Jennie and their three children Moses, Job and Lazarus continue to live primarily in the remote jungles laboring to see the entirety of God's Word translated into local languages. They are continually working to see tribal believers discipled and trained as teachers to their own people and other unreached areas.

D.S. Phillips sincerely believes that every believer in this generation has a responsibility to reach out and play a part in seeing each and every tribe, language and people group reached for the glory of God. It is his sincere desire that God will use his story to remind our generation that God is still doing incredible things in the deepest, most remote and unreached areas of this world for His own glory and that we have the awesome and exciting privilege of being a part of it.

More information about the Dao tribe and the work D.S. Phillips and his family are doing to spread the Gospel in Indonesia can be found at:

sjphillips.org

Also Available

from D.S. Phillips

The true story of a young couple who stumbled across a fierce, murderous, stone-age people group in the remote jungles of Indonesia only to find that they were the fulfillment to prophetic dreams given to the tribe long before their arrival.

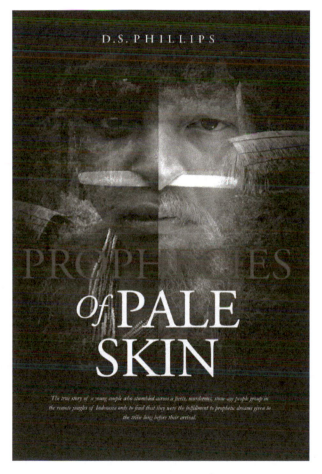

In *Prophecies of Pale Skin* you will be both challenged and inspired as you read about how a young couple was changed by the hardships and victories they experienced in living among the Dao tribe. You will see how these foreigners were inspired by the prophecies, dreams, beliefs and culture of that remote people group and also how the tribes people themselves were changed by the prophecies that the young travelers carried to them from the other side of the world.

Get the first chapter for free at propheciesofpaleskin.org
Or pick up the ebook or paperback online or through your local bookstore!